THE AUTISM RELATIONSHIPS HANDBOOK

How to Thrive in Friendships, Dating, and Love

Joe Biel and Faith G. Harper, PhD, LPC-S, ACS, ACN

Microcosm Publishing
Portland, Ore

THE AUTISM RELATIONSHIPS HANDBOOK
How to Thrive in Friendships, Dating, and Love

© 2021 Joe Biel and Fath G. Harper
© This edition Microcosm Publishing 2021
First edition - 3,000 copies - March 23, 2021
ISBN 9781621066194
This is Microcosm #485
Cover by Lindsey Cleworth
Edited by Elly Blue and Lydia Rogue

To join the ranks of high-class stores that feature Microcosm titles, talk to your local rep: In the U.S. **COMO** (Atlantic), **FUJII** (Midwest), **BOOK TRAVELERS WEST** (Pacific), **TURNAROUND** (Europe), **UTP/MANDA** (Canada), **NEW SOUTH** (Australia/New Zealand), **GPS** in Asia, Africa, India, South America, and other countries, or **FAIRE** and **GIFTS OF NATURE** in the gift trade.

For a catalog, write or visit:
Microcosm Publishing
2752 N Williams Ave.
Portland, OR 97227
https://microcosm.pub/htra

Library of Congress Cataloging-in-Publication Data

Names: Biel, Joe, author. | Harper, Faith G., author.
Title: The autism relationships handbook : how to thrive in friendships, dating, and love / by Joe Biel & Faith G. Harper, PhD, LPC-S, ACS, ACN.
Description: Portland, OR : Microcosm Publishing, [2020] | Summary: "Ever since he came out as autistic, people have been contacting Joe to share their stories and ask questions. The most common question by far: how do I find a romantic partner? Dr. Faith G. Harper, author of Unfuck Your Brain and Unfuck Your Intimacy joins autistic publisher and author Joe Biel to offer hard-won guidance on a wide range of topics about friendships, dating, and romance and answer a ton of questions. What do you want out of a relationship? What is the difference between flirting and harassment? How do you have a fun date and get to know someone when eye contact and prolonged conversation aren't your strengths? How do you change a casual acquaintance into friendship or dating? How do you express your needs and make sure you're hearing your partner when they express theirs? How do you maintain a healthy, happy long term relationship? Autistic readers will find valuable answers and perspectives in this book, whether you're just getting ready to jump into dating, seeking to forge closer friendships, or looking to improve your existing partnership or marriage"-- Provided by publisher.
Identifiers: LCCN 2020024278 | ISBN 9781621066194 (trade paperback) | ISBN 9781621066224 (ebook)
Subjects: LCSH: Autism. | Autistic people----Social life and customs.
Classification: LCC RC553.A88 B522 2021 | DDC 616.85/882--dc23
LC record available at https://lccn.loc.gov/2020024278

MICROCOSM · PUBLISHING

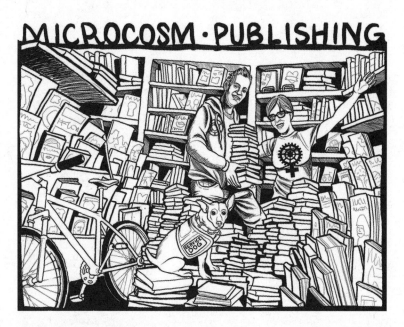

MICROCOSM PUBLISHING is Portland's most diversified publishing house and distributor with a focus on the colorful, authentic, and empowering. Our books and zines have put your power in your hands since 1996, equipping readers to make positive changes in their lives and in the world around them. Microcosm emphasizes skill-building, showing hidden histories, and fostering creativity through challenging conventional publishing wisdom with books and bookettes about DIY skills, food, bicycling, gender, self-care, and social justice. What was once a distro and record label was started by Joe Biel in his bedroom and has become among the oldest independent publishing houses in Portland, OR. We are a politically moderate, centrist publisher in a world that has inched to the right for the past 80 years.

Global labor conditions are bad, and our roots in industrial Cleveland in the 70s and 80s made us appreciate the need to treat workers right. Therefore, our books are MADE IN THE USA.

CONTENTS

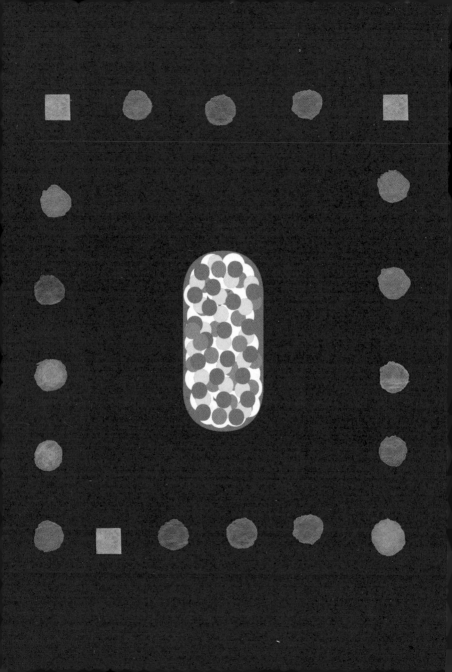

INTRODUCTION

Welcome. We wrote this book to save the lives of autistic people.

That's not overinflated ego on our part. In 2017, the *American Journal of Public Health* reported a study that the average autistic person only lives to be 36 years old. The leading cause of death is suicide because of social isolation—nine times more likely than our allistic (not neurodiverse) peers.

Relationships, including friendships, are the biggest protective factor against dying by suicide. Other people in your life help you curb those feelings of loneliness and isolation while helping you keep pace in the rhythms of life with other people. Other people may not be able to fix everything that you are struggling with, but they can love and support you while you struggle.

Additionally, those of us who are neurodiverse are twelve times more likely than the general population to be the victims of abuse from parents, teachers, and other authorities. These experiences lead to substantial trauma and problematic attachment styles that get in the way of seeking relationships and friendships even though healthy relationships are the best medicine to help us to better be supported and understand these events in our lives. Not to mention, having other people around in our emotional lives keeps us safer because others who care about us are watching and protecting us.

Often this treatment manifests in the form of anxiety, depression, anger, addiction, maladaptive problem solving, trust issues, and trauma triggers that might not be helpful in the present for solving problems. Sometimes, when we need the most support, we lash out at others from fear of rejection. Pushing someone away before they surely will push us away is far safer for us, according to our traumatized brains.

Joe was diagnosed with autism at 32 and mentors half a dozen autistic young people. The number one topic that they ask about is dating and relationships. They want to know how to judge someone's character, why their friends keep scattering, how to express interest, how to know if someone likes them, and how to know if someone has the same values as they do, i.e. is "a good person." Of course, they rarely like Joe's advice because these are not simple areas of personal growth. When you find stories in the first person throughout this book (e.g., "I had this experience"), that's Joe talking.

Faith is a therapist who works with numerous neurodiverse individuals. Two of her special focuses are trauma (which a lot of autistic people experience because of how neurodiverse people are treated in society; you can read about coping with trauma in her bestselling book *Unfuck Your Brain*), and relationships (which you can read about in the sequel, *Unfuck Your Intimacy*). She also happens to have a (now adult) child who is neurodiverse and would sob at night over how difficult and exhausting it was to understand other human beings, which of course made her want to punch the entire planet on a regular basis. Hopefully all of this means that she has a lot of wisdom to offer here, for the parts of your dating / relationshipping / intimacy that have to do with autism, the parts that have to do with trauma, and the parts that are hard for all humans (because sometimes it's nice to know that the allistics are struggling, too).

If you're autistic or think you might be, this guide is for you. If you're single and happy with it, or single and don't want to be, or dating, or in a relationship that's happy or unhappy or you just aren't sure how any of this is "supposed" to work, or between relationships, or etc… this book is for you.

If you aren't autistic, but you think maybe someone in your life is, this book might help you to understand them better and teach you how you might improve your relationship.

A common joke in autistic circles is about the horrors of the allistic (non-autistic) disability. It goes roughly like this:

Person A: "Everyone around me has a disorder that makes them say things that they don't mean, disregard rules and structure, not know how to ask a question in a format that will provide them with the answer that they seek, fail to focus on topics that are important to them, have unreliable memory, constantly express strange bits of coded language and hints, and creepily stare at my eyeballs."

Person B: "So why do people think *you're* weird?"

Person A: "Because they comprise over 98% of the population."

Allistics are neurotypicals, who comprise the vast majority of people, those featuring "brains with nothing interesting or worth noting about them." While the oddity of the allistic is a source of endless amusement and fascination for our continued study, we almost always have to coexist with them. So in this guide we are going to focus on how to successfully form bonds, develop friendships, go on dates, and even form longtime relationships with these weirdos.[1] This book is also intended to be useful for autistic people in relationships with other neurodiverse individuals.

Autistic life, perhaps even more than allistic life, is about learning from a series of experiences. The primary difference is that for most autistic people, our biggest problem is social isolation, loneliness, and the resulting death by suicide because of how difficult it is to live in a world not designed for us. So let's look at ways to form lasting relationships, prevent social isolation, and ultimately save lives!

1 Our editor advised against calling them "boronorms."

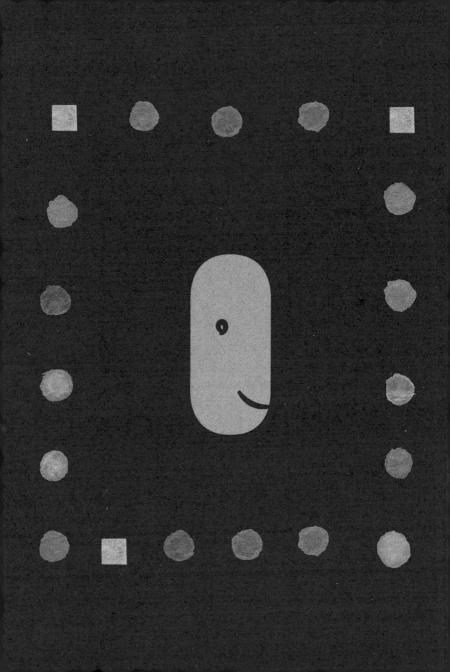

PART ONE:
YOUR RELATIONSHIP WITH YOURSELF

INTRODUCTION
WHAT IT MEANS TO BE AUTISTIC (AND WHY THAT IS AWESOME)

Autism is not a new diagnosis. The number of people receiving the diagnosis has gone up, not because the rates of autism are increasing at warp speed, but because we are getting better at recognizing autism for what it is. The news was full of Chicken Little type reporting in 2014, when the autism diagnosis rate jumped from 1 in 88 to 1 in 68. Was it a new vaccine on the market? Nope, we just got better at diagnosing and defining it.

Generally autism involves variations on nine pieces of criteria:

1) We have 400% more resting brain activity than most people. Our senses and our brains notice more stuff. Sometimes that's light or heat or visual detail or flavor. Some doctors call this "sensory issues." Others call it the "Intense World Theory." This is why autistics have filled vital roles in history like inventors, composers, problem solvers, and developers.

2) We get exhausted because of all of this information. This results in stress symptoms, meltdowns, and a real need for alone time.

3) People who are not autistic operate in nuance and code (you know, essentially being cryptic, irrational messes who make no sense). Autistic people don't, which leads to what autism specialists undersell as "difficulty socializing."

4) We operate based on a series of complex and elaborate rules that get more complicated every day. Life is like a to-do list and we check a lot of boxes because the structure helps us manage all that brain activity overwhelm. Autism professionals call this "needing to adhere to a stringent routine."

5) It's hard to understand what other people are thinking or feeling unless they tell us in plain, exact language or we have a lot of history together. For some reason, most people are very uninclined to do either of these things. Autism professionals call this difficulty understanding others "Theory of Mind."

6) We do stuff repetitively both in the micro and macro sense. When I was a child I spent hours feeling the texture of a torn-up, dirty blanket. It brought comfort to my small, chaotic world. Naturally, it was destroyed in the washing machine when my neighbors got lice. Now I play with my hair or rub my fingers together. There was a fad around autistic people using fidget spinners for this purpose a few years ago. Most of us open and close our hands repeatedly or make repetitive motions of flapping our appendages. Doctors call this stuff "stimming" as it helps us to relax and be present in our bodies. I'm fairly sure that it's the only socially *unacceptable* coping mechanism. Not convinced? Go to a bar and watch how socially acceptable drinking is. Still not convinced? Go on the internet and look how much of it is about screaming at one another and calling complete strangers "garbage." Compare how all of *these* coping strategies affect other people and how harmless stimming is in comparison.

7) We are fixated on cool stuff. When I was five I liked dolls and action figures. Then I loved Legos deeply. For a year I glued together models of dinosaurs and recited every fact about them. Soon I abandoned that for Dungeons & Dragons

but that was a little too social for me so I found punk rock and memorized all of the facts about that. Then I became a publisher 25 years ago and fortunately was able to find a way to turn that into a new, exciting adventure every year. I often realize that I've been talking about this stuff for way too long to someone who is politely disinterested and doesn't know how to kill the conversation. Autism professionals call this "Persistent, intense preoccupations."

8) Periodically we find ourselves in a social place full of people where no one will talk to us. We try to spark conversation but people don't want to engage. Sometimes we apply for a job and have better qualifications than the job requires but they hire someone else anyway. The missing piece is that we cannot see how others see us. We cannot see the outside view of how our amalgamated choices have bad optics. In short, I look like a sloppy mess who is a bit of a loose cannon or wild card. We cannot see this because we see each of our choices as separate, individual things rather than the composite that they create. On rare occasions I ask someone what happened and they point out a series of very specific and seemingly irrelevant things that I did and said. They explain to me that these things are immature and that other people notice these patterns and make judgments about me as a result. Sometimes these polite, patient people also explain to me how my composite choices actually drive me away from my goals. For example, perhaps I want to buy a new stereo but I keep loaning money to strangers who need it. Or I want to become the President[2] but I keep taking low-tier jobs in food service. It's hard for autistic people to break goals down into actionable steps and see their

---

2 Who am I kidding? No reasonable person *really* wants to be the President, anyone good at the job arrives at it kicking and screaming.

actions how neurotypicals (NTs) do. Autism professionals call this "Difficulty with Executive Function."

9) We have an even greater capacity for empathy than the average population, we just don't access it through the same means as others. In short, we feel things much more intensely but connecting the dots with others' experiences to our own can be difficult. We tend to have very dull mirror neurons, meaning we are not great at neuroception, the brain's ability to detect the intent of others without conscious thought. So we struggle to read and experience other people's feelings, body language, nonverbal communication, and mental states. People who don't experience neuroception are often read as cold, withholding, or in other ways emotionally withdrawn, disconnecting, or even abusive. It's very hard for NTs to understand that we aren't doing this on purpose and because of that autism is frequently equated with sociopathy. In practice it's the opposite. A sociopath is very emotionally perceptive and thus adept at manipulating and exploiting the emotions and weaknesses of other people while an autistic person can often be completely clueless as to the feelings or motives of others. While an autistic person does not mean to or realize that they hurt others, the impact can be just as great. We are lacking a window into other people's worlds until they tell us what it's like to be them. It often takes some very plain language to make others' experiences and feelings relate to our own. As we age, we learn to intellectually mimic these skills through recognizing patterns and behaviors, but this is an extremely draining amount of emotional labor for us to perform. It's also important to point out that our struggles with neuroception mean that we not only struggle to connect and relate, we are at higher risk to be taken advantage of by others. The instincts

that tell others to move away from dangerous people are tied to neuroception, and we simply don't have the skills.

Most people confuse anxiety and social awkwardness with autism, but those are merely consequences of an ableist society. Others think that if they are introverted and find the tags of their clothing irritating, that they must be autistic, but there's a bit more to it than that. If you aren't sure but suspect that you or someone close to you is autistic, ask the person the following questions:

- Are you overly sensitive to stimulus, such as touch/smells/ sounds/sights/tastes?
- If you don't have time to process these stimuli, do they lead to feeling overwhelmed or having meltdowns?
- Do you have trouble instinctively understanding other people's sense of humor or emotional expressions?

If you said yes to all three, a good next step is to take a few online tests. If those tests indicate autism as well, research what options are available for definitive diagnosis locally. This can be complicated for financial reasons as well as lack of access. Adult diagnosis can be difficult to obtain because psychologists are now apprehensive about over-diagnosing autistic adults. So many autistics merely look at the facts and self-diagnose. This seemed strange at first, but I understand that living in a city where I could obtain an official diagnosis for a few hundred dollars is very different than most people's circumstances. Faith has regularly worked with individuals that were told over and over by other clinicians that they were "probably autistic" but they never assigned the diagnosis themselves until they saw her. In addition to the fear of over-diagnosing and the stigma associated with getting any mental health diagnosis, most clinicians get very little training in neurodiversity in their graduate school programs and, depending on where they are, finding mentoring and post-graduate training can be difficult. Faith isn't excusing anyone, she's just speaking to how the problem is systemic and there are very good reasons for giving up and self-diagnosing and/or bouncing from professional to professional while seeking support.

Cis women and girls who are autistic statistically have greater social adaptability skills so they are particularly good at masking symptoms and blending, making them less likely to be noticed or diagnosed. They tend to be more socially accepted for a number of reasons; most notably they have better hygiene, adapt faster to appropriate behavior, and exhibit social anxiety less visibly. In short, autistic cis women mask better than cis men do. Presumably this is because cis women are raised to be hyperaware of patriarchal and sexist expectations from society at such a level that even a neurodiverse brain will learn the lesson. Similarly, due to patriarchy, autism in women can be dismissed as shyness, which is socially acceptable, while men who act shy are ridiculed. There isn't research about transgender and enby people masking, but from our extensive experience, enby and trans people are not particularly skilled at masking.

Some people are born with certain inherent privileges based on their identity and appearance and the cultural values of their society. Normally this privilege is simply because these groups comprise either a majority of the population or that people like them hold all of the power in society. Lots of other marginalized populations—non-white people, queer and transgender people, women, individuals with disabilities both visible and invisible—face exponential discrimination, insensitive remarks, and expectations to do more emotional labor in order to be treated as an equal. The struggles of being autistic aren't the same as other marginalized groups, but those of us who are neurodiverse are doing extra relational labor on a daily basis. Respect the work that you do. It's exhausting to be different in a world that demands that you either conform or set yourself off on an ice floe. You are a badass. Similarly, understanding that other marginalized people are experiencing similar mistreatment can be important to consider and respect.

HISTORY

The word "autism," which has been in use for about 100 years, comes from the Greek word "autos," meaning "self." The term describes conditions in which a person is removed from social interaction—hence, an isolated self. Eugen Bleuler, a Swiss psychiatrist, was the first person to use the term. He started using it around 1911 to refer to one group of symptoms of schizophrenia. We've known about autism for over 100 years, but originally thought it a form of childhood-onset schizophrenia, which sorta made sense at that time. Autism was believed to be a thought disorder where one sees/hears/smells/feels things that others do not and believes things that are empirically false. A lot of the soothing behaviors associated with autism were thought to be a response to internal stimuli. We know better now.

In the 1940s, researchers in the U.S. began to use the term "autism" to describe children with emotional or social problems. Leo Kanner, a doctor from Johns Hopkins University, used it to describe the withdrawn behavior of several children he studied. At about the same time, Hans Asperger, a scientist in Germany, identified a similar condition that's now called Asperger's syndrome.

But even through the 1960s, treatment professionals still thought autism to be a form of schizophrenia. Once there was a realization that autism was a different form of neurodiversity that did not include symptoms of a thought disorder, treatments actually got worse, focusing on punishment-based "curative" strategies, like electroshock therapy and LSD. It wasn't until the 1980s that treatment professionals started looking at behavioral strategies and adaptations to learning environments to help autistic people live their best possible lives in a neuronormative world. And rest assured, you will still encounter plenty of people that believe we should be punished into behaving like neurotypicals.

For the pop culture understanding of autism there's *Rain Man*, who convinced the world that if we really were autistic, we would be lying face down on the floor performing experimental calculus equations in our heads. I do experimental calculus for fun sometimes but I don't often do so while lying face down on the floor. The floor is typically dirty and cold, so that would be ridiculous.

AUTISM AS A SUPERPOWER

As Dr. Laurent Mottron proved in 2011, autistic people concentrate more of our brain's resources on visual processing and less on planning and impulse control. That explains why, in 2009, he found that we are 40% faster at problem solving! All people take in 11 million bits of information every second of the day but can only consciously attend to about 50 bits. We are much better at determining which bits are relevant to the matter at hand. We also have excellent memories, both from long-ago events and recalling details that allistics gloss over. An *Onion's* parody news video depicts an autistic reporter covering a fatal train accident. "Luckily there was no structural damage caused to the train," the actor proclaims, before reciting specific details about the train.

Autistic people are born without the instinctive ability to emotionally interface with 98% of the population. This is a difficulty that can be overcome. To be social and autistic is to do *more* emotional labor than allistics do. For example, to prevent ourselves from upsetting someone we often need to observe and respond to facial expressions, body language, subtle remarks, coded speech, and group dynamics; things that allistics can literally do without thinking.

The *Journal of Autism and Developmental Disorders* found that autistic people are also tremendously creative thinkers, focusing on many different properties of objects they interface with and the versatility of each. When shown something, the study participants could immediately come up with an extensive list of uses far outside of the intended functions. And as you develop critical-thinking strengths around your meaning and purpose, you'll be doing things that you care about and love. Others can see and recognize this, even if it's not what you mean to communicate. Creative thinking will demonstrate your ability and value to others, even if they had dismissed or overlooked it in the past.

It's annoying when allistics say "you don't seem autistic." It can help to realize that they actually mean "I know very little about autism." If you respond by asking a few journalistic questions like "What do you mean?" or "Can you explain?" they often realize how little they know. This is how neurotypicals initiate conversation. They want to know a little about what autism is or how it functions. More importantly, they cannot fathom what autistic life is like.

If you're feeling a little spicy, develop a witty response like "you don't seem to know much about autism." When someone makes an insensitive or ignorant remark about autism or your identity, try to give them the benefit of the doubt that they don't know how to ask for more information. Insulting the other person too harshly or harping on your hardship will only prevent you from educating them and maintaining the relationship. So don't go too far... unless these aren't concerns for you. In that case, people will talk about how you behave and ultimately, you need to make a conscious decision if you want to deal with this. It might not always feel like it, but you have your own strengths that they don't. And ultimately, leaning into your strengths, even if they aren't the ones society expects from you, is what makes it possible to have authentic interactions and relationships with others.

HOW TRAUMA FUCKS UP OUR SENSE OF SELF

WHAT IS TRAUMA?

Trauma is so common for autistic people that it clouds the ability for psychologists to diagnose adults. Trauma is, again, a product of how we are treated by allistics and society at large.

Trauma is an injury to the nervous system caused by horrific events that we did not have the capacity or support to heal from. When you don't adequately process the trauma to understand what happened and why, the event becomes hard coded into your brain and affects your experience and behavior even after the danger has passed. Why does the brain do this?

Your brain's job, first and foremost, is to keep you alive. Your brain is hardwired to protect you, and in order to do so it's going to err on the side of caution. The brain uses shortcuts (psychologists call them *heuristics*) to problem solve and make decisions quickly and without expending significant effort. So rather than performing a complicated set of if/then checks, the brain tries to keep you safe through a series of shortcuts it has developed based on all of the previous times (priors) that it sensed danger. Of course, this means it'll misfire and it won't always do a great job at assessing what is actually a threat and what isn't. Erring on the side of caution makes protective sense, right? And our brain's protective responses often end up doing the opposite—getting us into unhealthy patterns of behavior that hurt us and others.

Here's how the brain's threat assessment system works. The brain looks like a bunched up mass of overcooked pasta, right? The brainstem is the part where it starts to untangle itself from the rest of the noodles, straightens out, and transitions into your spinal cord. The brainstem is our fundamental survival tool. While cardiac muscles regulate basic needs like breathing in and out and the heart pumping, the brainstem controls the rate, speed, and intensity of these things. So it will ramp up for a panic attack, for example, as if to say *pay attention; we might be dying.*

Being alert, being conscious, and being aware of our surroundings are all brain stem tasks. When the brainstem is registering pain or panicking, it floods the prefrontal cortex (PFC) with a bunch of neurochemicals that change how the PFC operates. The PFC is the part of your brain in charge of *executive functioning,* like problem-solving, goal-oriented behaviors, and managing social interactions according to "appropriate" expectations. When our brain stem senses danger, based on our priors, the behavioral actions of the PFC become *fight, flight,* or *freeze.*

- Fight interprets your best course of action as *beat their ass before your ass gets beat.*
- Flight determines *get the fuck out of here! This isn't safe!*
- Freeze means *if you don't respond at all, maybe they will go away.*

These are essential survival tasks when something dangerous is going on, such as when cavemen came face to face with a prehistoric housecat the size of a small sedan. The amygdala, the brain's fear processor, says "I remember the last time this happened, it really hurt, which was bad!" And the brainstem tells the prefrontal cortex "Let's get out of here so we don't get hurt again!" So we run away. Or we fight back. Or we freeze up and play dead and hope the situation passes us over.

Being able to assess threats and respond appropriately is a necessary survival skill and isn't problematic in and of itself. But when our threat system is activated continuously or activated in very extreme circumstances, it can end up staying turned on. A trauma is essentially anything that overwhelms our ability to cope, and if we don't achieve resolution and healing from traumatic events our brains continue to respond from this trauma-activated state. Which can lead to these survival responses being frequently misapplied to situations where we feel under attack but aren't facing any real threat. All kinds of things can feel threatening... like a final exam or a bullshit work deadline or wordlessly walking past a stranger on the street.

One study linked incidences of autistic people being violent to instances of unresolved past traumas.[3] Our experiences determine our expectations for the future, and thus form our reality. Our brains are fed a certain amount of raw data that is processed to determine conclusions about what is going on around us. They generalize and err on the side of safety. The autistic brain is both more susceptible to being taken advantage of and has trouble noticing larger patterns, so we are doubly susceptible to trauma misleading us. That raw data from our brain is not made available to our conscious selves—only the conclusions that our brain draws from it are. And these interpretations of that data inform our reality. If your worldview is interpreted through a lens of unhealed trauma, you are more likely to respond to the present as if you are reliving a past trauma. For example, if you have been attacked by a stranger in a dark alley, you may believe that this is a common event. If your previous employer went out of business suddenly without warning, you'd be concerned that your present employer will too, despite no evidence of this happening. If a friend abruptly ended a friendship in the past, it can feel like this is what friends do and you'll expect it in all future relationships because it's difficult to see how the circumstances are different now. It is through these same devices that, if you were to see a black and white photo of a banana, your brain will interpret it to be yellow because of every banana that you've seen previously.

---

3 https://pubmed.ncbi.nlm.nih.gov/27236173/

It's important for us to recognize that we are unreliable narrators about the facts of our own realities. Our sensors become too subjectively attuned and you are more likely to remember the emotional experience of how something felt, rather than the material facts of what happened. Accepting this can be very difficult because your reality is so convincing. When others disagree, it can feel like they are trying to overwrite our emotional experiences with their own.

Similarly, if you have formative experiences at a young age, these can downright define how you see the world. I was physically abused from a young age so I expected that I would be treated this way for my entire life. Consequently, I put myself in situations where this could happen because it did not occur to me that I had other options. This is exactly how a tripped threat assessment system left unhealed turns into a trauma response.

For these reasons, it's vital to understand how past traumas can affect friendships and relationships now. With some practice, you can take a few steps back and access your conscious, thinking brain. Then you can start to take apart the situation. Why are you feeling this way? Is it because of the present or the past? It's important not to be oblivious and taken advantage of but also be able to understand why you won't continually relive your fears and worst moments.

HOW TRAUMA AFFECTS RELATIONSHIPS

One of the big impacts of trauma is it makes it difficult to love yourself. It's too easy to internalize and repeat the negative voices from the hurtful experiences of your past[4]. There is a sneaky and mean idea in our society that you have to love yourself in order to have other people love you. That's unfair, because we all experience times in our lives where we are unhappy with who we are. And that doesn't make us

---

4 To learn how to fix traumas in your brain, check out Dr. Faith's first book *Unfuck Your Brain*

unworthy of love. We are never, ever going to tell you you can't have a relationship if you don't love yourself, pinky swear.

It can be much easier to form healthy relationships when you have healthy attachment to other people. But there are numerous impediments to this based on your prior life experiences.

Starting in 1958, psychiatrist and psychoanalyst John Browlby developed the theory of attachment styles, initially for children and their attachment to their mothers. This theory has since become understood to inform other relationships through adulthood, largely because of the way that we've been treated as children. The styles are:

- **Secure attachment:** You are happy to be reunited with someone who you feel close to and sad when they leave your company. You freely go about your business, unafraid that they will secretly leave you

- **Dismissive-avoidant attachment**: Wary of strangers because of past treatment, you generally feign ambivalence about the company of people that you are close to. You ignore them as they come and go but the whole thing is an act to hide your inner distress. Essentially you have the protection of their company but don't risk being rebuffed.

- **Anxious-preoccupied attachment**: Your comfort is based on proximity to people that you feel close to and you are highly distressed when separated but feign ambivalence upon their return. You are wary of strangers at all times. Expressions of anger and helplessness are often used to take control of your behavior. Others are understandably frustrated at your constant seeking out and then resisting contact. This attachment style is often a result of abuse as a child which made it difficult to maintain adult relationships.[5]

5 McCarthy and Taylor (1999) https://www.semanticscholar.org/paper/Trauma-as-a-Contributor-to-

- **Fearful-avoidant attachment (a.k.a., disorganized)**: Afraid to express emotion because doing so was punished during formative years, this is now masked through tensed muscles and hunched shoulders. As a result of past violence, your relationships are ruled by fear with seemingly contradictory behaviors, such as laughing while you brace to be punched. Yet you still seek comfort from those you feel close to, however fleeting it may be.

The more you learn to like yourself, the easier it is to be around other people. And the more you like yourself, the easier it is for other people to enjoy your personality and companionship. Based on your past experiences, this can be a difficult and gradual process. It certainly was for me. You're probably cavorting around a sea of hateful and insulting statements in your brain that you've internalized over the years to form your self-image. And I sympathize with you. It's unfair that others' treatment of you is now your responsibility to resolve, but ultimately that's beside the point. This is something that you must deal with.

In the last chapter of this book, we'll give you some more tools for dealing with trauma, and protecting yourself from being traumatized in future relationships.

ADDICTION

Similarly, because of the sheer volume of trauma that autistic people experience and how confusing it is, we are particularly susceptible to addiction.

I am a member of several adult autism groups and there are quite a few people, including myself, that have been labeled as addicts in the past. Addiction is much more common among autistics. While there isn't more than preliminary research[6] about this subject (and very little research about autistic adults in general), the anecdotal evidence

Violence-in-Autism-Im/28d60193a22b9fc6c37dd06a5c5823cc8c8b0160?p2df
6 pubmed.ncbi.nlm.nih.gov/26903789/

is that autistic people use substances for different reasons, sometimes making recovery easier to achieve once we make that choice. Instead of replacing a relationship, as in standard addictive behaviors, autistic people are frequently trying to make peace with our brains. One man, when told that doing heroin would kill him, stated he wanted to die, and thus cultivated a years-long pattern of use only to discover that this was a pretty long goodbye. "Heroin will kill you" was yet another allistic lie. So he quit. And recovery included learning to be at peace with and even learn to like his brain. He no longer had any interest in dying or heroin. This isn't to say that recovery is super simple if you are neurodiverse, but Faith has found that, if a certain action makes more sense than what they are currently doing, autistic individuals will give everything they have toward change.

Once we learn to like our brains, we no longer have a need for the scaffolding of an addictive behavior—whether it's drinking, gambling, or heroin. I'd urge you to apply this science to creating the life that you want for yourself. *Pursue your meaning and purpose every day and use your brain to double down on how to do this more effectively.* You'll find that your brain, when pursuing things that you care about—no matter what they are—is much more efficient than the allistic brain.

Similarly to trauma and addiction, most autistic people suffer intensively from depression and anxiety. These four problems co-occur with autism so frequently that they confuse and cloud adult diagnosis. Essentially, it's difficult to separate the ways that our personality has been shaped by how we've been treated (because of our autism) from the autism itself. Getting to know yourself, practicing accessing your thinking brain, and understanding your motivations are a good way to get started. If there are parts of yourself that you are unhappy with, just knowing that is a good start. To better understand changing your behavior or if you're getting stuck, we have numerous other books, including *How to Be Accountable, This is Your Brain on Depression, Unfuck*

Your Anxiety, This is Your Brain on Addiction, and *Unfuck Your Brain* that further explore each of these issues individually.

Use the fact that you are 40% faster at problem solving to your advantage! Tackle the problem of becoming the person that you want to be, first through unpacking who you are and why, then breaking the project down into manageable steps. This is where secure attachment comes from—being comfortable in your own skin. Wade into situations that have been a little uncomfortable in the past until they are more and more comfortable. Take notes about when you react, panic, repel people, or are no longer expressing yourself in a way that you feel proud about. For most of us we weren't raised in a way that met our needs or allowed us to turn out healthy or functional. So we are, in turn, forced to become our own parent.

Let's start by getting in touch with what's important to us.

DEVELOP YOUR VALUES

Values clarification exercises help us determine what we find the most important in life. And how we describe ourselves and perceive ourselves (if we are doing so congruently) is usually a reflection of our values and how we are living them.

When your behavior is not in keeping with your values, your self-image begins to break down. If there is a disconnect between our values and our actions, this is a chance to pay attention to that experience and set yourself back on course.

When we face a difficult decision, we have four sets of guiding principles:

- *personal values* that are unique to ourselves
- *institutional values* that are supplied by schools, governments, or employers
- *group values* that are inherited from people or a community that we identify with
- Similarly, *societal values* are things like the age of consent, submitting accurate paperwork at your school or job, and respecting your neighbors by not owning too many chickens.

Most people have personal values like honesty, compassion, bravery, or respect for the agency of others. It's important to figure out what we value rather than what we were trained to value, or value because our families did while we were growing up. This can be challenging to define for ourselves.

Sometimes respecting institutional, group, or societal values can be important even if you don't agree with them. But it's important to simultaneously recognize your own values, especially if you cannot act in accordance with them at this moment. Aligning with our own values adds a sense of mission to the "getting better" part of unfuckening.

Many people don't have a language to articulate their values. Get a sheet of paper and make a list of your own values now. Brainstorm for about twenty minutes. If you're having trouble thinking of them, search online for sample lists. You can make a separate list of institutional, group, and social values you were raised with and compare the lists.

UNDERSTAND YOUR FEELINGS

To understand what you need from other people, you first need to be in touch with your own feelings.

Many autistic people are frustrated with the fact that they have feelings (feelings aren't very logical), have trouble accessing their own emotions, or simply become frustrated with the feelings that they are having and how they are an impediment to what they want in the moment. The first time that I was sat down in counseling and was asked what I was feeling, I was literally unaware that I even had emotions. This is not uncommon.

The reason for this is that 85% of adult autistics have alexithymia, the difficulty identifying and describing our own and others' emotions. Fortunately, while this behavior may not be instinctive for you, it can be learned. At the same time we feel and react to our feelings much more intensely than allistics.

If you have trouble understanding your feelings, look at pictures of yourself to see what you actually look like in various situations and figure out what physical comfort looks and feels like for you. For some people this takes a lot of time, observation, and subtle realization to really see your own expression. Paul Ekman's book *Emotions Revealed: Recognizing Faces and Feelings to Improve Communication and Emotional Life* can be helpful if this exercise is unfamiliar. It contains hundreds of photos of facial expressions and explains the emotion that is being depicted.

Here are some skill building tips when you are still having trouble defining your feelings or you find that your instinctual reaction or behavior isn't serving your goals:

- Recognize when your emotions are activated in some kind of way, in either a joyful or uncomfortable way. You don't have to figure out the exact feeling all the time, especially right away. Starting with a recognition that your body is happy or unhappy with something is a very good start. Feelings are just information from our body, encouraging us to do more of one thing and less of another, right?

- List the emotions that you frequently experience, such as joy, frustration, anger, sadness, amusement, confusion, annoyance, excitement, satisfaction, coziness, disappointment, despair, or surprise. We'll have a more complete list with exercises in the workbook that accompanies this book.

- Describe to yourself how you know that you are experiencing these emotions. You will often feel a disconnect or a betrayal between your body and your mind as values from your upbringing are instilling feelings that you don't want to have because they aren't consistent with how you see the world now. If you were taught that you should always respect authority figures but one routinely insults you, your feelings will tell you when your actions are not in line with your values. Sit with your feelings and process what is going on in your body and mind. This is how you work them out of your life. If you're still having trouble, there is an exercise for understanding the physical, visual, and mental manifestations of the primary emotions in the accompanying workbook.

- Make a list of events or behaviors that frequently cause those emotions, rating each one 1-10 on the scale of unpleasantness.

- Figure out what you appreciate or need when experiencing each feeling.

- Ask for what you need from those that care about you.

You can apply these same skills to learning to recognize others' feelings, if that's something you have trouble with. Understanding your own and others' feelings are equally important parts of a relationship or friendship. Otherwise, the relationship will only serve the needs of one person while both participants disregard the needs of the other. If you're having trouble, revisit the above skills. If you want more, check out Dr. Faith's *Coping Skills*.

FIGURE OUT YOUR BOUNDARIES

Most people inherit a lot of baggage, responsibility, and cultural "rights and wrongs" from their family of origin. For example, even if their family members are terrible at getting along with each other, if getting along with each other is a value of the family, then adult children will continue to live by those values and often impose them on others who have different priorities and family circumstances.

Becoming an adult means shedding all of this and making your own choices for what's best for you. And dealing with the consequences of your choices. This is where boundaries come in. You get to make the rules that you will live by, hold yourself to them, and ultimately benefit from them.

Boundaries protect things that are yours—like your body, beliefs, choices, time, money, feelings, or investments—from being taken away from you without your consent. Think of consent as your enthusiastic affirmative and boundaries as politely declining something that doesn't interest you right now.

Each person's boundaries are a set of rules about how they behave and how others get to treat them. We can hold different boundaries rigidly, loosely, or flexibly, depending on our histories and decisions. For autistic people, understanding our own and others' boundaries has special challenges. In Faith's previous book *Unfuck Your Boundaries*, she wrote about how allistic people take in 11 million bits of information every second of the day but can only consciously attend to about 50 bits. Because autistic people experience 400% more resting brain activity, it can be difficult to focus on the relevant details because your reactions can be confusing or overwhelming. This is the core of the autistic experience. For this reason, we need to focus on our needs and wants, to know the difference, and to make decisions accordingly.

Needs are non-negotiable things that we require to survive, like food, sleep, shelter, respect, agency, warmth, and safety. Wants are things that are nice to have, but not necessary, like chocolate, a new video game, designer clothing, eating out, romance, and everything else. Most people spend years of their life finding that it's easier to get their wants met than their needs and then having trouble prioritizing their needs as a result. By accepting these things, we make these arguments in our heads that our wants *are* needs—or at least are justified. This is always done at a cost to our needs and to those around us. For this reason and more, it's important to know the difference. Similarly, when they affect other people or we need accommodation, we need to discuss our wants, needs, desires, boundaries, and personal space as frequently and as matter-of-factly as people talk about sports, video games, celebrities, or movies. It'll be awkward and uncomfortable at first because people aren't expecting it but it gets easier with practice.

HOW DO BOUNDARIES WORK?

What's normal and acceptable to one person might be abhorrent to another. For example, I once made a very lucrative living being tickled on film with very few clothes on. Many people that I meet find this idea shocking and horrifying. But for me it was great because I wasn't making compromises or giving power away to the boss. The amount I was paid per hour was much higher than other work, which allowed me to better meet my needs without abandoning any of my values.

Autistics are taken advantage of disproportionately more often than the general population. We are perceived as gullible and easily recruited into service for others so we must stay vigilant throughout our lives. People will try to make you commit crimes or they will touch you in ways that you don't like. They will try to make you say or do things that you don't mean, or that don't resonate with your authentic self. By knowing your boundaries in advance, you are prepared before you are in the middle of a tense situation.

Our feelings are completely our own, and we shouldn't blame others for them. We can, however, ask others for different behaviors that better respect our boundaries. This skill works in regular communication and stays in place even if your convo has leveled up to conflict level. Staying with ownership of your own feelings completely shifts away from the blame game. In short, you feel how you feel and that gives you information about both this situation and how you've been treated in your past. At the same time, the other person behaved how they did and is responsible for that. You can't change the past but you can request that people behave differently in the future. If someone consistently does not treat you in the way that you've requested, it means they are violating your boundaries and they are not a safe person to have in your life. The way that they respond to these boundaries is very revealing. For example, if someone becomes angry when you ask them not to touch you or to deliver their requests in a more respectful way, this means that they have become accustomed to not being held accountable to their own behavior.

Boundaries are important because letting someone do something unpleasant that you don't want does not make them like you more. Having no boundaries does not mean that other people will let you do what you want to them in return. In fact it does the opposite: it shows them that they have power over you, and that you are likely to allow them to do what they want to you with an increasing frequency and unpleasantness. So create and hold a boundary, especially as people test it.

Even when you really love someone, sometimes you need to set a boundary when you want to be left alone or just don't want to talk. Sometimes it's something like "Please don't read my diary" or "Please don't go in my room when I'm not home." If you experience sexual attention that you don't want, set a firm boundary like "I'm sorry. I'm not interested in you that way right now." If you are female, femme presenting, or gender nonconforming, you may find that you frequently have to turn away inappropriate advances and people trying to take advantage of you. The most illuminating way to better understand a relationship is to see how that person responds to your boundaries.

Similarly, other people have boundaries and have a right to create and hold them. Sometimes this will be very clear, like "do not touch me." Other times, allistics express boundaries in extremely subtle ways, like hesitating when you ask them a question or not answering the question that you asked. Often you will have to guide them that it's okay to express their boundaries to you and that you want to respect them. And that, honestly, speaking their boundaries as concrete as pavement is far better for you than dancing around it. You can encourage them to do so by checking in regularly and asking clarifying questions.

Often our intentions do not align with our impact, meaning that you can hurt other people's feelings even when you were trying to do something nice for them. Even when our action seems completely unrelated, what matters is how the other person feels about it. For example, I once told someone I was dating that they were very strong. I meant it as a compliment but it made them feel insecure because they thought I was calling them fat. It was a pre-existing issue that had nothing to do with me but my words still hurt, so I do not to compliment them about that any more. Similarly, sometimes strangers assume that any attention will lead to nefarious motives. Like, if we are asking for directions, they assume that we are next going to ask for money. This is further complicated because allistics mistake their feelings for their reality; part of their disability is that the narrative created by their feelings is actually more important to them than the events that actually happened or taking the opportunity to understand them differently. Being concerned about allistic feelings is still our responsibility in these scenarios. You do this by believing in and respecting their expressed needs, even if you don't understand. If you hurt someone's feelings, you should apologize, learn from it, and try not to repeat it, even if it doesn't immediately make sense. Asking someone that you trust can help to understand what went wrong.

Some people are pushier than others. Someone who doesn't know how to get their needs met will often act like a bully. Bullies make people agree with them. Non-bullies respect differing opinions, actions, perspectives, and needs. Don't be a bully. Listen to others and respect them, but don't let them do anything to you that makes you uncomfortable.

Autistic people have tendencies towards always saying yes or no right away, even when you might need or want to really take the time to access how you feel about each decision. Sometimes you'll know immediately, like if someone is touching you in a way that makes you feel uncomfortable and you need to shout "Stop it! Get your hands off of me!" Sometimes you'll have regrets later and need to express them. Here's a sample script "I felt _____, when you _____, and what I want in the future is _____." Sometimes it's a positive but usually if you are having this conversation it means that someone that you trusted unintentionally hurt you and probably doesn't even know it. So you get to tell them, taking responsibility for your emotional response, and both grow from it together.

People often mistake boundaries as a chance to prevent our feelings from being hurt in the first place; as a way to make us feel loved and protected. But this is a counterproductive strategy. Once you understand that you can hurt other people's feelings, when you aren't intending to, a common response is to try to avoid delivering information that would hurt their feelings and expect them to treat you the same way. These are both boundary violations because they invariably result in lies, lies of omission, and other kinds of not disclosing how we truly feel. Other people cannot prevent or rescue us from situations that we find painful. We need to take responsibility for our own feelings and how we let others treat us and expect them to do the same.

As adults, even when a situation is unfair or we are in extreme pain or we are wholly incompetent at taking care of ourselves or feel unable to cope, we are still responsible for our own emotional well being. Asking for help from people who love us is important but it cannot solely be what we rely upon to keep us safe all the time. Just because we are bad at handling something does not make it someone else's responsibility. We need to eventually learn how to take care of ourselves.

There are many other kinds of violating boundaries of yourself and others that you may not realize immediately on your own:

- Not speaking up when something is important to you
- Not prioritizing your own opinions or emotions
- Giving more than your emotional or physical limits
- Not communicating when you've reached those limits

- Giving without asking for what you need in return

Here's a longer list of boundary violations that people do to each other, from Faith's book *Unfuck Your Boundaries*. Some of these things are more long-term harmful than others, but they're all good examples of things to avoid doing to others and not accept others doing to you:

- Sexual abuse
- Physical abuse
- Unwanted touch (including touch at times someone doesn't want to be touched, in ways they don't want to be touched, and in places the person doesn't want to be touched)
- Entering someone's living space without consent
- Cutting in front of someone in line without consent
- Not cleaning up one's own mess
- Using another person's property without consent
- Not returning or being late to return property (even if it was borrowed with consent)
- Not adhering to time agreements (being perpetually late or uncomfortably early)
- Taking control of someone else's child when their parent or guardian is present
- Moving in to live with another person without permission
- Smoking in front of others or in their living space without their consent
- Asking personal questions outside of the depth of the relationship
- Asking others to justify their actions or viewpoints when neither impacts us
- Giving feedback about someone's behavior when it doesn't affect us

- Listening to the phone conversations of others
- Reading others' diaries, letters, emails, or private messages
- Sharing secrets or things told to us in confidence (gossiping counts here)
- Assuming the feelings of others
- Assuming the reasons for others' behavior
- Assuming others' thoughts
- Making demands instead of requests
- Expressing "advice" or "constructive criticism" when it was unsolicited and/or is offered for the sole purpose of hurting the person who is the recipient of the comments.
- Treating someone in a condescending way (talking to people as if they were a child or slow to understand)
- Judging others
- Sharing personal information about oneself without checking out if the hear-er wants to hear it
- Using abusive language
- Misgendering someone
- Using transphobic or trans-exclusionary language
- Using racist or racially stereotyped language
- Asking for excessive or inappropriate favors
- Expecting a favor exchange (giving favors assuming favors will be given in return)
- Triangulating (trying to use a third party to control someone)
- Pushing past someone's "no" or any limits they have set
- Helping someone without first asking if they would like help
- Interrupting someone while they are talking
- Trying to force adults to live by someone else's moral and ethical standards

- Intruding at a gathering, such as joining others at a restaurant without being invited
- Continued pursuit of a relationship with someone who has indicated that they are not interested (regardless if they had maintained a relationship in the past)
- Indulging our desires at the expense or harm of another

One caution as we look at these: There's something all brains are wired to do called the *fundamental attribution error*. When we mess up and violate someone else's boundaries, we attribute our actions to the situation at hand (whether this is a reasonable justification or not). When another person messes up and violates our boundaries, allistic people attribute it to that other person being a fundamentally terrible person. Autistic people are inclined to make excuses for the other person's behavior, or even ignore the violation, hoping it goes away. Unfortunately, this isn't a courtesy and merely communicates that we allow ourselves to be treated this way. Autistic people often have the additional problem of missing how the pattern of our behavior creates a composite experience for others over time.

This is the brain's default way of thinking and until we develop an awareness of it and learn how to think through it, it's difficult to form relationships that are substantial and lasting. Autistic people are not immune to the fundamental attribution error, but we have an easier time bringing ourselves back to other possibilities. Adding a level of critical thinking, consideration, and awareness allows us to pay attention to the details of each situation we encounter and make better decisions about whether someone is a true threat to our safety (and we will be talking more about red flags in that regard later in this book) or just a blundering human that will do better in the future if we bring our issues to their attention. In most cases when hurt is caused, a little bit of fault belongs to each person. So working together is the only way to make things better for people in the future.

Now that you've read this list, the next step is to start noticing these boundary violations. From there, you'll be in good shape not to do them and replace them with other behaviors, as well as speaking up or making changes when people do them to you. This is the most important step in becoming the director of your own life.

MAKING BOUNDARIES

Twenty minutes spent creating and defining your boundaries will save you *years* of misery. These are feelings and ideas that you know are right for you and come from yourself, rather than from other people's ideas. Don't feel guilty about these things. It will feel hard in the moment sometimes but ultimately everyone will be happier in the long term.

Think about each of these questions. You can have more than one answer for each one, and your answers can change over time:

Basic human dignity boundaries:

- What are your needs? (e.g. for people in your life not to deny your autism)

- What do you need out of each week? (e.g. to be left alone while you sort your pills, three square meals)

- What do you want your ideal week to look like? (e.g. rigid schedules including fave video game after dinner)

- What do you need from a friend or partner after school or work? (e.g. to listen while you tell them what was exciting that day)

Home life boundaries:

- How many minutes a day do you want to spend alone? (e.g. 720 divided equally in between all social activities)

- What kind of living conditions do you need at home to function ideally? (e.g. for things not to be moved from where I placed them previously)

- What do you want out of a home? (e.g. to come home to people who are understanding and supportive of difficult experiences)

- Do you feel comfortable where you live now? Why or why not? Can you make your own home more comfortable or do you need to find a new one? (e.g. yes, because when there is a disagreement we can talk about it rather than having someone else's needs prioritized over my own)

Friendship boundaries:
- How much time do you want to spend each week with friends? (e.g. two hours divided across four days after school)

- What do you need out of a friendship? (e.g. someone who actively listens and takes fault when they hurt my feelings)

- What do you want out of a friendship? (e.g. I relate to their experiences and interests)

- What regrets do you have about your behavior in past friendships? What can you now learn from these experiences? (e.g. my insecurity pushed me to try and "prove" myself too hard)

- For friends you have now or have had in the past, what works and what doesn't work in those friendships? (e.g. balancing equal time spent listening and talking)

- What activities do you like to do with friends? (e.g. play with board games, talk about dinosaurs, listen to punk records)

- What would be your ideal friendship mix? (e.g. a few close friends vs a larger social group)

Relationship boundaries:
- Would you like to go on dates? If so, what would you like to do on dates? When would you like to go on dates? Where would you like to go on dates? (e.g. see a movie on Friday night and then talk about it for 20 minutes afterwards)

- Would adding someone to your life impede your ability to be comfortable? What would it take for comfort to happen, both now and with the addition of a partner? (e.g. defined hours/ places of socializing and time alone)

- What regrets do you have about your behavior in past relationships? What can you now learn from these experiences? (e.g. I asserted my needs too forcefully rather than simultaneously identifying others' boundaries)

- What do you need out of a romantic relationship? (e.g. someone that I feel unequivocally understood by)

- What do you want out of a relationship? (e.g. someone to share new experiences with)

- What would you *never* do to preserve a relationship? (e.g. violate my body or deeply held values)

- How many minutes per day would you like to spend talking to your date? (e.g. 240, with three breaks so as not to be overwhelmed)

- How many hours per week would you like to spend in each other's company? You can also change your answers as other circumstances in your lives change. (e.g. fourteen, across four days)

- What's your preferred form of communication with your date or partner? (e.g. writing down the most important things or communicating based on a system that you create together)

- How many nights per week would you like to spend sleeping over at each other's homes? (e.g. two so that it doesn't disrupt my routines too much—I'm easily distractible)

Sexual boundaries:
- Is sex something that you want in the first place? (it's okay if not; social pressures can lead us to believe that it will be pleasurable when it's really not for us)

- When do you want to be sexual with your partner? (e.g. after work, first thing in the morning, before bed)

- Do you prefer a predictable sexual routine or to be surprised? (e.g. sometimes consistency and expectation are best, sometimes the appeal is in not knowing)

- What feels good? (e.g. no penetration; just hands)

- How do you like to be touched? (e.g. firm touch rather than light fingers gliding)

- How do you want your partner to escalate sexual contact? (e.g. through verbal questions that I nod to or decline)

- What feels good to you and your partner? (e.g. talking about the sex afterwards when we listen and share)

Boundaries at work/in groups:
- What accommodations do you need to ask for at work? (e.g. a quiet place, social distance, lack of smells/visual distractions)

- Do you want to form friendships in these environments? (e.g. not really but maybe a few people)

- What makes you feel confident? (e.g. smaller groups within a larger group)

- How do you best maintain clear headed thinking? (e.g. taking breaks, time alone, stimming)

- What aspects lead to your best creativity? (e.g. quiet, discussion, lack of distractions, reviewing your inspirations)

HOW TO ENFORCE YOUR BOUNDARIES

Boundaries can and should change over time as you figure what works for you and what doesn't. If you are in the process of establishing and holding better boundaries with someone for the first time, it's going to feel emotionally charged since it's all weird and awkward and new for everyone involved. Having a bit of a recipe will help a ton. Try this one. Add extra garlic if you're feeling sassy. Changing boundaries later can be more difficult, since there are existing expectations in the relationship.

This is your BIFF script for setting boundaries with a new person, or with someone who is having trouble respecting your boundaries. In our example, your boss just sent you a scathing message about losing the keys to the dumpster at work while sending a lot of accusation and blame your way:

Brief: Don't give any extra info. Don't over-explain. The more you write or say, the more fodder you are giving the aggrieved party for their battle, yeah? Let's say you got an angry missive from your boss, accusing you of jacking the keys to the dumpster. Instead of writing an eight-paragraph defense, try a brief, factual response: "I clocked out two hours before closing last Thursday, so I didn't carry out the garbage that day and I never used the keys."

Informative: Don't focus on their incorrect statements, focus on your accurate ones. No sarcasm, no negging, no remarks about the other person's personality, ethical choices, etc. We are looking to end the conflict, not throw down about who the real dumbass in this scenario is. In the same work example, you might add the information, "In order to refresh my memory, I double checked the calendar. I wasn't the person who closed that day, it was Xander."

Friendly: I know, it doesn't seem fair that you have to be nice when someone else is showing their ass. The best way of coming out of the conflict unscathed is to not match hostility with hostility. This doesn't mean fake nicey-nice... just civil. You are far more likely to get a neutral response, if not a positive one. Going back to the work example, you could phrase it as something like "Hi, Sarah! Xander and I did both work last Thursday, but I clocked out early because it was so slow and Xander closed by themselves, so I don't know where the keys to the dumpster ended up."

Firm: Be firm without being threatening. Don't make comments that can invite more discussion (e.g., "Let me know if you have any questions" or "I hope you agree that..."). Back to Xander the key-stealer? You could close with "I wish I could be of more help, hopefully Xander will be." Think like Forrest Gump. As in "that's all I have to say about that." If you need to get a decision from someone and can't end the discussion here, another feature of "firm" is offering two choices so you don't have continued over-discussion. "Would you like to talk to Xander or would you rather I take care of this?"

UNDERSTAND YOUR SEXUALITY AND GENDER

A major component to your own identity is your gender and sexuality. Do you identify with the gender you were assigned at birth? If so, do you relate with the socialized interests and stereotypes of that gender? Are you only attracted to people of a different gender? If you say "yes" to all three, you won the lottery and the world will not fight you on this issue. You can skip ahead to the next heading if you want. But at least take from this section that most people aren't so lucky and are subtly fighting these battles secretly in their heads every day. It's your responsibility to be respectful of them.

If you didn't say yes to all three questions, that's okay too. Almost nobody does, but yet we all face tremendous pressure to conform to these stereotypes and behaviors. Boys are punished for playing with dolls (even the really cool and interesting ones) and feminine boys or tough girls face strangers—not to mention people close to us—going to great lengths to push us back in line with social norms. They will call us insulting names or worse. For men, as little as wearing pink or enjoying women's clothing better (again, far more interesting) can be met with violence. Still, these are not great reasons to restrain who you really are and the stakes for doing so are tremendous. Not identifying with your birth-assigned gender can put you at an even greater risk of suicide. Not because you are inherently messed up because you are not cisgender, but because you are having to perform a role you were assigned that doesn't fit you. And many people around you will have very strong feelings about you sticking to that script.

Autistic people are roughly seven times more likely to be gender noncoforming, transgender, or queer than our allistic peers. This is notable. In numerous groups that I've been a part of, cis people—

those whose gender identity matches that of the body that they were born into—have been the minority. In allistic circles, this would be an incredible statistical anomaly, but for autistic people, perhaps as a result of having to build our identities and taboos from the ground up, we are much more likely not to identify with the gender of our birth body. Some people even feel like their gender fluctuates from time to time or don't identify with any gender at all. By and large, this level of self-realization and actualization can be as important as your autism diagnosis because it allows you to become comfortable with a vital component of who you are.

A lot of individuals who treat being transgender as a mental illness point to this fact as evidence that being trans is an autistic perseveration. To which our first response is "so what? let them transition!" and our second thought is *correlation is not causation*. It's just as likely, and makes a ton of sense, that anyone who is neurodiverse is less interested in and invested in social roles and is far more likely to recognize they don't fit into their assigned label and will therefore protest it.

Like all things, gender is a social construct that is performative at many levels. Gender is probably more flexible for autistic people because it's another in a series of many social performances. Everything from our choices of clothing, pitch of voice, expected topics of conversation, passivity or assertiveness, and interests are the social dance that allistic cisgender people are programmed for. Andres Bravo, a 26-year old autistic trans man, explains "We learn how to be our gender through social immersion, cues, and pressures which are often missed if they're indirect. For example, women can openly talk about menstruation around other women, but the mood of a room changes if she brings the topic into a mixed gender setting, which might go unnoticed if she is on the spectrum."

Bravo continues "Same gender relationships are much more forgiving with fluid gender expression. Whatever 'feminine' social qualities I have are usually written off as 'queer' traits because I'm a man dating another man. Before transitioning I presented myself as a woman with 'masculine' qualities. At the time I was in a relationship with a woman, it was assumed my androgyny came from being a lesbian. Strangers and friends would much sooner attribute androgynous traits to queerness rather than questioning a person's gender."

If you are unsure about your sexuality, pay attention. There's a certain shame imposed by allistics on sexual desires, especially among people that they deem as "disabled." So rejecting that shame and getting in touch with yourself can take some conscious paying attention. What excites you sexually? What about it excites you specifically? Are you uninterested in anyone at all, sexually? That's fine too and there are lots of others like you. Maybe you want a romantic partner for reasons other than sex; merely someone to relate to, feel close to, and share your life with. You can be *asexual* without being *aromantic*. And you are not doomed to never have a relationship if that's the case, it just changes your dating pool.

Otherwise, think about who you are attracted to and why. Often, the earliest indicators are attractions to characters on television in our youth (Faith was very pro-Bowie in *Labyrinth* as a kid for what it's worth). Some people are attracted to more than one gender of person (if not all types of people). Being polysexual is often referred to as bisexual or pansexual or just plain old queer. The most important thing is being true to yourself and understanding how you feel without associating it with shame.

Gender can be even more complicated. Maybe you identify with the body that you were born into but just hate all of the social expectations. You are a woman who likes to have a shaved head, share opinions freely, and use tools to build things. Despite what people will impose on you, this is a perfectly acceptable way to express yourself, as long as it's honest and consistent with who you are. Some people have a more complicated path where surgery is necessary to change their body to become more like the way that they feel inside. There are literally infinite options available—far more than we could get into properly here. If you want a thorough exploration of this topic, check out *How to Understand Your Gender: A Practical Guide for Exploring Who You Are* by Alex Iantaffi and Meg-John Barker.

Either way, these issues are complicated, vast, and confusing. You may not know the answers to any or all of them immediately. That's okay too. We encourage you to explore how you feel about these things, both alone and in conversation with people that you trust. Don't jump into any major disclosures or changes right away. Spend some time really understanding how you feel, which aspects are your own and which come from outside pressure, and then make the decisions that are right for you. Then talk with current or future partners about how they can best respect you.

LEARN FROM YOUR MISTAKES

Everything in your life is stuff that you practice. And you will make mistakes! A mistake is anything hurtful to yourself or others where you could have acted differently to produce a different outcome. The important thing is not to give up and feel like a failure, but to take notes each time and apply the lessons to your future activities.

When I was a kid, no one knew that I was autistic. Everyone—including myself—knew that I was weird and unlike my neighbors, friends, classmates, and peers. But without the label of autism, I wasn't segregated. I went to school and was mostly placed in regular classes, where I sometimes did very well and sometimes was bored and well below average, despite being hyper intelligent. I met all kinds of kids and lived in a neighborhood where I made friends, most of whom I'm still in touch with 40 years later. These relationships could be confusing and weird. Some of my "friends" teased me for saying the wrong things, wearing the "wrong" clothes, or liking different music than they did. When I responded by teasing them about their music, clothes, or statements, they got angry and defensive with me. The same rules did not apply. If I stared at someone out of curiosity, that was rude. If someone stared at me because I was weird, that was somehow okay. I came to learn that there was a social pecking order and some people did try to be my friend because they saw me as less than and able to be dominated. Others saw me as an equal or recognized that I wasn't going to attempt to dominate them. When I asked people out on dates, I was often laughed at but sometimes—to my delight—I was accepted. Of course, I'd still be heartbroken when my date cheated on me or otherwise hurt my feelings. The idea that autistic people don't have feelings is pathologized and projected onto us so furiously that periodic reminders that we *do* have feelings and that it is okay are important.

Even more so for autistic people than most, building relationships involves a lot of learning, and thus some rejection and pain. A successful autistic person has the freedom to make all kinds of mistakes on their own without being stifled by their parents, partner, or loved ones. In a popular meme, the mother of an autistic child asks an autistic adult for advice on employers hiring "special needs" kids. The autistic adult suggests focusing on jobs that the child is excited about and qualified for. Not understanding the wisdom of the statement, the mom locates another mother of an autistic child who refers to five employers who knowingly hire "special needs employees." The problem is that putting the kid into the "special needs" category is telling them that they are "less than" rather than focusing on their talents. Nobody wants to be chosen on the grounds that they are inherently broken or out of pity. Parents have an understandable inclination to prevent their kids from experiencing rejection and pain, but these things are ultimately how you learn from your experiences.

Most autistic people who are diagnosed early are either painfully neglected or stifled with every second of their lives overmanaged for fear that they might harm themselves. Many people in your life may try to shelter you—friends, lovers, dates, teachers, bosses, and peers. When you discover this is happening, look at their motives and have a clear conversation with them, explaining that this information is what helps you to learn from your experiences. And no matter how old you are, it's never too late to start taking control of your own life. It's okay for other people to state their concerns about your choices or your life, but ultimately the decisions have to be your own.

One real-life example shared with me is about a young autistic girl who found a caterpillar and was fascinated by it. She put it into a jar to show her mom. Her mom taught her how to care for it and to put grass, sticks, and plants in the jar for the caterpillar to grow healthy and strong. The caterpillar began acting strangely and the girl's mom explained that it was creating a cocoon. Feeling parental ownership of this young caterpillar, the girl watched as the caterpillar began metamorphosis to become a butterfly. She kept a watchful eye on the cocoon but became concerned. A small hole appeared in the cocoon but it was apparent that the caterpillar was weak—struggling—and could not get out. The little girl, worried about her caterpillar and with the best of intentions, obtained a pair of scissors and cut a large hole in the cocoon. The butterfly immediately climbed out! The girl was relieved. But all was not well. The butterfly was bloated with underdeveloped wings. Its body never healed and the wings never grew. The butterfly never learned to fly and lived out the remainder of its life crawling around helplessly.

The girl talked to a biologist who explained that building up strength in the cocoon is ultimately what eradicates excess fluid from a butterfly's body into its wings. Otherwise, the butterfly can never fly. You also need room to learn from painful growth.

A popular story on *This American Life* focuses on a blind man who has learned to ride his bike and function in the world through echolocation. He endlessly clicks his tongue and—like a bat—pays attention to the sound echoing to determine his proximity to danger. Of course, this means that he has fallen down hills, walked into poles, and received numerous injuries across the years. But ultimately, these experiences led to his independence. He can function on his own and those scars are ultimately lessons.

Learning to navigate in the neurotypical social world means we'll make a lot of mistakes. Frequently, events like these feel like failures. It can be very difficult to focus on the applicable lessons rather than just the failure itself. So when something doesn't work out the way that you had hoped, wait a few weeks, then schedule some time to think and write about what you were trying to achieve. Try to look at all of the variables and see where you might have acted differently. Talk to someone that you trust. Find the lessons and continue to refine your approach until you achieve your goals.

In my experience, autistic people who are the most functional, independent adults live in the grey area between having lots of support and having none at all. You need to have supportive people in your life, and also enough space to make your own mistakes. It's painful but it's exciting and fun and—more importantly—it's the only way forward. It's how we learn to painstakingly take care of ourselves socially. It's how you learn to judge the character of people in order to make sure that they are safe to allow into your life; that you can trust them.

You will make mistakes. You will hurt people and get hurt. You will trust people that you shouldn't and misunderstand vital communications at times. This is part of the human experience, autistic or allistic. It's part of life. Others who shield you—even with the best of intentions—from these painful experiences are stagnating your growth and preventing your independence. Struggle is growth. Mistakes teach lessons.

The shortest route to ride my bike to work is the interstate, but that doesn't make it the *best* way. When I was younger, this still seemed like the *best* way, but really it's not that great at all. I would likely get run over by someone that doesn't expect me to be there. What makes sense to you may not make sense to other people. Similarly, if your feelings get hurt when you get rejected from asking someone on a date, it doesn't mean no one wants to date you. It contains secret codes and vital information to unscramble for doing things differently next time. It can still be difficult to learn these lessons. Some situations will seem very different to you from previous ones but others will only see the similarities. If you keep choosing to ride your bike on the interstate, you can't blame other people for the outcome. Relationships are similar but more subtle. If multiple partners tell you that you are too rough sexually, you need to reevaluate your approach, not continue your habit with new partners. When you're in any painful situation take some time to make a list of lessons from it.

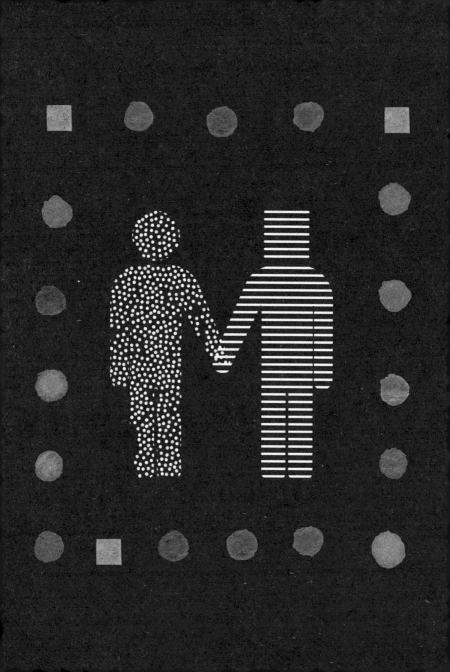

PART TWO:
YOUR RELATIONSHIPS WITH OTHER PEOPLE
INTRODUCTION

A relationship is the space between two people. It's usually built and characterized on shared experiences, mutual respect, or a combination of the two. A relationship can be everything from a friendship to a marriage to the way that you relate to your parents, co-workers, classmates, or people on the street—to everything in between. It can be friendly or hostile or sexual or scary or violent or funny or joyful or many of these at once. You can tell different things to your mail carrier than to your childhood best friend or your mom. And you'll receive *very* different reactions from each one. Each type of relationship has a different role in your life. Friendships usually aren't sexual or romantic. The same skills apply so it can be confusing that different rules and expectations apply. And that a vital part of relationships is respecting the other person.

Relationships are about the reward, satisfaction, and feeling of emotional proximity. Essentially, each one revolves around the value of feeling understood. So the complicated parts are being authentic to yourself and knowing what a healthy amount of disclosure looks like.

In September 2019, Humans of New York profiled a young, heterosexual autistic man. He described his autism as a terrible social impediment that made it impossible to meet women. He claimed that his only sexual experiences had been with prostitutes. Standing next to a cute woman at his bus stop, he Googled "how to approach women" and fell into the manipulative world of the Pick Up Artist (PUA) movement, where men are taught how to exploit women's emotions.

This set of instructions led him into a dark world of socializing with other Pick Up Artists and thinking that he'd found the answer he was looking for. Today, he claims to have over one thousand phone numbers for women and the feeling that there was finally something in his life that he was good at. The write-up ends with his explanation of how to give half-compliments so the women chase validation and him admitting, "Of course it's manipulation, but why should I care? I've been manipulated so many times in my life."

Numerous autistic people claimed that Humans of New York was using this person's story to frame all autistic people. But I see this issue a bit differently. People like this are why I wrote this book. Yes, this man is knowingly manipulating and carrying on the hurt that he has felt instead of responding with empathy. The PUA movement is mostly composed of non-autistic men who have also struggled to "get the girl." This individual, like most men who engage in this behavior, had fallen through the cracks of not having a positive, fulfilling way to form substantial relationships that might nourish him even more than chasing hookups. It's easy to vilify someone when they act badly because it allows us not to look at the larger picture that allowed this situation to develop. Besides, I'd urge you not to view someone's worst behavior as being definitive of their character.

Imagine if this young man (or any PUA) had a feminist community of other autistic people who taught him how to form relationships through bonding instead of manipulation. Rather than seeing him as a role model who is rewarded repeatedly for hurtful behavior, we can come to see him as someone lacking role models who can help him achieve his goals and come to feel understanding and, gradually, comfortability in his own skin.

More important, I'm willing to bet that this young man never found what he was actually looking for: emotional proximity and intimacy with other people. There are many ways to find what suits you, but having lots of sex with various partners doesn't replace actual human connection. There's nothing wrong with it if everyone is consenting but it sure doesn't make you feel understood and the emotions are fleeting. So if intentional relationships are something that you are just embarking upon, friendships are a great place to start.

And like all relationships, friendships have to be mutual, meaning that everyone is getting something out of it, even if it's different things. So things like manipulation and deception really inhibit relationships, especially in the long term. Part of that is considering what you want or enjoy from each relationship in your life. Hopefully the first part of the book gave you some idea of what you're looking for in different kinds of relationships.

Remember how we mentioned how many autistic people are also gender and/or sexual minorities? It's okay to not want to have romantic or sexual relationships either, or to have limits around what you want. You might still need or want to have more experiences before you really understand your own wants and needs or to understand what the people in your life are dealing with. More mistakes will lead to more experience and thus a better understanding of what someone is asking or expecting of you.

Once you know what you want and need from different kinds of relationships, you'll be able to talk about it, and encourage your friends, dates, or partners to talk about what they want and need in turn. One of the major disabilities of allistic people is that because they are the majority, they will expect you to want the same things that they do. Your advantage is that because you've already had the experience of unpacking all of their coded language and social expectations, you can talk them through this as well. For whatever reason, once you've established some emotional proximity, allistic people tend to enjoy conversations about needs and expectations in a relationship. Most people don't like you to offer hard observations but when you are in a relationship and some trust is formed, people will often marvel at what you observe. And when you talk about your relationship dynamics, it doesn't tend to feel like an attack because they interpret the conversation as being about *you* rather than about *them*. These conversations feel profound and thought provoking to allistics because they bring up things people haven't considered before. And more importantly, it's fun to put all of this emotional labor to use and have someone else recognize your value. Besides, a conversation like this creates more emotional proximity.

But sooner or later you'll need to have "the talk." You do not suffer from allistic disability. You are different and it's probably not going to be news to the people in your life. They have probably established that your brain works differently and have maintained the relationship.

This seems counterintuitive at first, but when you leave others to guess about your diagnosis, they will assume the worst possible scenario when you have a disagreement, or they witness behavior that doesn't make sense to them. Brains are assholes like that. Remember: *emotional narratives are more important to allistics than facts.*

A friend of mine was told by her parents not to tell her boyfriend that she's autistic, because they believe that people will take advantage of her if they know. This doesn't make any sense to me. Someone that close to you already knows that you are autistic, even if they don't know the word for it. They witness your daily behaviors and habits and, lacking the language, they still accept you how you are. Giving them the tools to work through issues and conflicts will make your relationship longer and more harmonious.

Andres Bravo explains, "At first it was scary to tell people I was autistic. Many allistics equate autism to a mental illness or a disease. Autism is nothing to be ashamed of. This is something that makes us unique, like being born left-handed instead of right-handed. Remembering this has boosted my confidence whenever I disclose to someone new. Folks pick up on your radical self-acceptance and tend to react with an open mind."

People in your life probably won't be surprised and ultimately won't care too much about the label. They care about you and your lived experience and how society treats you. Ultimately someone that loves you will not think differently of you because of this. However, the risk in disclosing is that people will *deny your diagnosis*. This can be very hurtful and confusing for someone to tell you that you aren't autistic when you firmly know that, well, you are. This is usually because people know very little about autism. Sometimes these conversations can be salvaged and you can educate someone but sometimes it can mean the end of the relationship if the other person has wrong-headed ideas about autism and wants to impose their emotional narrative over your expertise and experience.

These conversations can be uncomfortable but just because something is uncomfortable doesn't mean that it's a bad idea. That's just your brain telling you to be careful. When someone asks you a question that makes you uncomfortable, ask yourself "What is the meaning and purpose of the overall conversation?" If what is being asked of you fits within that frame and you don't feel compromised by offering the information, it may create greater emotional proximity to share.

Before we get too far ahead of ourselves though, let's talk about various ways to make sure that you are successful in various kinds of relationships.

BUILDING BLOCKS FOR ANY RELATIONSHIP

While every relationship is different, we're going to spend a few minutes looking at what is the same in all relationships. By thinking about these things from your own experience and what you know about the other person, you can dramatically increase your chances of success!

UNDERSTAND AND RELATE TO THEIR FEELINGS

To understand other people's needs you need to be in touch with their feelings. This is why you must actively practice listening, empathy, and understanding when they share their feelings.

Sometimes we feel so much empathy that it is deafening. Other times we cannot understand someone else's experience so we feel nothing about it. Sometimes things that are really upsetting for others have no apparent impact on us. For these reasons, it's difficult to instinctively predict or understand other people's feelings. Researcher Simon Baron-Cohen has depicted autistic people as largely devoid of empathy, further setting back popular understanding of our internal experience.

There are two different kinds of empathy. *Affective empathy* is the instinctive ability to experience others' emotions like a contagious disease. *Cognitive empathy* is the conscious drive to recognize someone else's emotional state from their speech, behavior, and nonverbal communication. Autistic people are particularly gifted with affective empathy but tend to have less cognitive empathy.

Consequently, researchers Coralie Chevalier and Robert Schultz believe that autistic children might not feel as "rewarded" by the act of engaging with others as allistics do, making us less motivated and, over time, less able to see the internal experiences of others. But this also means that when we *are* motivated, we are quite capable of empathy and do it "unexpectedly" well. Why is that unexpected? Allistics have a very difficult time understanding lived experiences outside of their own. In a more recent study, autistic people were found to have an equal ability to recognize regret and relief in others as neurotypicals do. Individual mileage with empathy may vary, however.

When my grandfather died, I didn't experience much emotionally. I may have been too young to fully grasp it or perhaps it was the fact that he was mean to me more often than not. Perhaps I didn't understand death yet. I was five or six years old. Instead, I reacted with pure, calculated logic and performed emotions because I knew that was the correct thing to do in that circumstance.

Conversely, when my dad died twenty years later, I was very sad but did not feel the need to perform emotions for the benefit of the allistics. Instead, I socialized with my friends that I hadn't seen in years and recalled old times. In ways, this too was a calculated decision: to be a rock when others were breaking down emotionally. It didn't feel insincere, but for most of my life I felt like my emotional expression was for the benefit of others. This is the autistic mask, or at least one form of it. My dad was a genuinely kind person who was abused for my whole life and I learned much of this at his funeral as well as other details I had never known about him. I was taught my entire life that he was the "bad" and "selfish" guy in our family and it wasn't until then that I realized that he was the victim. So it was deeply affecting, but I realized that my scrutinizing of others' words and actions at his funeral was actually reflecting my own emotional state about losing him and wondering what the "appropriate" reaction was.

As you can see, emotions are confusing and complicated for autistic people. So we often defer to the allistics around us for cultural and behavioral norms. Sometimes that gets us into trouble.

Psychologists describe autistic people as "displaying rigid patterns of behavior." We often can't see this in ourselves, but allistics can see it in us. And it tends to tell them how we value their emotional states. I'd ideally have the same three identical meals every day, with the food eaten in a particular sequence and the same routine hour by hour. This often involves vegan mac and cheese, in case you are wondering. This would drive most allistics wild. Rather than seeing this as a statement of my own tastes, allistics tend to perceive the definitiveness of my tastes as shutting down the conversation, potentially excluding what they want. So when asked what you want or your opinion while making a decision, it's important not to be too definitive, and ask for the other person's input in return.

If you're really having trouble identifying someone else's feelings, it's okay to do the obvious thing and *ask*. "Are you feeling sad?" or "Did I hurt your feelings?" gives them an opening to disclose to you, you to respond and compensate for your actions if needed, and for the two of you to grow closer as a result. Oddly, sometimes the other person won't be very versed or in touch with their own feelings and prompting the question will cause them to falter. This is okay too, even if it's uncomfortable for a few minutes. Ultimately working through someone's feelings shows that you care and are invested in them.

Autistic people have a tendency to respond to people's emotions by trying to solve their problems. It's vital to remember that you don't know what's best for anyone... except yourself. You might have an elaborate, composite picture of your closest friends, and probably have some good ideas and advice for their issues. But when they tell you about their problems, unless they specifically ask you for your opinion or advice, they probably are only seeking empathy. They want you to echo back how painful and difficult their struggles are, and how exciting and powerful their successes are. Otherwise you are probably going to hurt their feelings and create a rift. If you do, that's okay. Just apologize, take a mental note for next time, and move on. Autistic or allistic, Faith teaches all her clients to ask the following when someone they love is in a difficult space:

> What would be helpful from me right now? Do you need time alone, do you want me to hold space so you can process out loud, or would you like my help in trying to solve this?

Sometimes you will hold someone in a higher regard than others, perhaps because they are a hero or someone that you respect. Maybe they've taken care of you in the past or you just have tremendous appreciation for what they apply themselves to. This can lead to outsized expectations and disappointments when they prove to be mortal and make mistakes. Think of them as someone who, like you, screws up sometimes. It can be painful and sad, but take some time to sit with these feelings and make a careful choice about how to react. As the guest on the podcast *Sagittarian Matters,* allistic counselor and astrologer Jessica Lanyadoo explained, "When we go straight to blame and punishment, we signal to everyone who is trying that if they aren't perfectly there they should have shame. Where we have shame, it fuels the worst of ableism, classism, racism, homophobia, and all of these things. Most people aren't experts in everything. If we don't have room to make mistakes and have a learning curve, we have a problem."

Having conflicts with friends feels bad but it's good exercise. It prepares you for resolving conflict, which makes people closer and stronger. Once it's resolved, you and your friend will both be more invested in the relationship *because* of the fight. It gives you a chance to practice explaining yourself and understanding how you feel about things. You don't need to agree but you need to respect each other and understand where the other is coming from. Otherwise, you both need to ask yourselves why you are friends and adjust the relationship.

If you're outraged at someone who has hurt you, coming at them with your anger isn't going to change their behavior or facilitate growth. Lanyadoo spells it out thusly, "When you're yelling at someone, they aren't listening. They are thinking of how to defend themselves." This is because yelling triggers the parts of the brain that makes the other person feel attacked.[7] And when we are attacked, it's a time that we should be defending ourselves. We're being attacked! Of course, not all attacks are equal and someone's response to being yelled at will usually escalate the whole situation. So slow down, and before you react be thoughtful about what information you want to impart and what information the other person is imparting.

There are two standout tendencies for autistic people in relationships even more than the general population. First, we tend to "scorekeep," making points for each time we do something that we consider thoughtful or nice for someone else and subtracting a point when they do things that we consider thoughtful or nice for us. There are numerous problems with this. For one, we can't know someone else's intentions. Perhaps they do many nice things for us every day that we don't notice or appreciate. Worse, when we withhold being nice to someone for the sake of the score, the relationship falls apart. And put blankly, scorekeeping isn't how relationships work. The best friendship is based on each person giving according to their ability, taking according to their need, and enjoying your time together in between.

Scorekeeping also leads to the other common problem: taking the moral high ground. Autistic people frequently tell me that they are going to be "the better person," meaning that they don't like how someone else is treating them and rather than distancing themselves, they chose to demonstrate "moral superiority." But nobody cares if you are the righteous party. It changes nothing. You aren't making a case.

7 Check out Dr. Faith's first book *Unfuck Your Brain* for some very extensive brain science around what's going on up there.

You are just setting yourself up to get hurt more. Ask for what you need instead. You might discover that the other person isn't trying to hurt you, but that you didn't understand a previous communication. On the other hand, intentions matter but so does impact. If someone repeatedly hurts you, you have to ask yourself some hard questions about why you continue to subject yourself to those situations—but don't punish them. You aren't their parent and it leads to an even darker place. Trying to push someone else to make desired actions is a boundary violation. People need to have free will as much as is possible, without judgment. Or as Jessica explains, "I deeply, passionately believe that if we are condemning and punishing—whether it's to ourselves, our heroes, or others—we become part of the problem."

Ask yourself: Am I behaving towards myself and to others in a way that is authentic and intentional? Am I compromising or cutting corners? Is my expression consistent with my intentions? Is it coming through to others? Am I hiding parts of myself? I have a certain idea of how I come across in my head but once when I heard myself talking on video, I was horrified. I sounded much more scathing, frustrated, impatient, and critical in my tone than I realized or intended. I didn't feel that way so it wasn't an authentic representation of my emotions either. Part of the allistic disability is that even when you tell them that you aren't frustrated but they think your tone sounds that way, they assume that you either aren't aware of your feelings or you are lying to them. This applies to any emotion that they take personally. They will often react to how they think you feel, rather than how you actually feel. So you are left with a difficult choice: trying to make them understand or changing your behavior to their way of doing things. In my case, I chose to revisit and change my tone to acceptable forms for allistics. This is controversial in autistic circles because if allistic people had greater acceptance for us in the way that we naturally behave, no change would be necessary for our autistic traits. But either way you choose, this fork in the road will pose a difficult struggle. I decided to make adjustments toward the bigger goal of maintaining relationships that were important to me. I don't consider it a form of inauthenticity, but instead me speaking a language that is not my first language. I'm bumbling about in French a bit, but if I'm living in France, I'm going to try my best. I also believe that doing so is noticed and makes it easier to request similar accommodations in return.

Conversely, if you are having trouble having empathy for someone else's position, imagine what it's like to be them. Think about their concerns, problems, background, and fears. If you're still having trouble having sympathy for someone that you care about, imagine how difficult their life was as a child or imagine that their grandma just died.

Once you've learned social rules, you need to learn when to break them. Lanyadoo points out her most profound wisdom: "All skills become liabilities when overused." And this is true. If we keep refining rules and skills around them, we will eventually paint ourselves into a very lonely corner. So think about that when practicing a specific skill that isn't getting you where you want to go. If you're still having trouble, revisit the skills for recognizing your own feelings from the first part of the book.

DEALING WITH HURT FEELINGS

Often, other people will get upset about things that have nothing to do with you. As I was writing this chapter, a white woman rushed out of a public bathroom, at which point a Black man standing near the door insisted that she was running away from him. A common experience for Black men is that strangers are afraid of them, simply for existing in public places. The woman returned to apologize and explain herself. The man proceeded to shout at her, insult her size, and say abusive things. His feelings weren't about anything that she had done; they were likely a product of his prior experiences and being mistreated elsewhere in his life. Hurt feelings are about impact, not intention. His hurt feelings were real even if she hurt his feelings by accident and didn't necessarily owe him anything. But also, his feelings didn't make his reaction acceptable or any less hurtful.

The woman later said that she knew she had undeserved privilege in this situation and realized that if she complained to staff, he would be removed, or worse, the police would be called, while she would be apologized to for the inconvenience. Sometimes there is nothing you can do because the other person just wants to fight. Sometimes, for your own safety, you can use a quick, "I'm sorry," rather than a more explanatory empathic one. This way you can convey that you didn't mean to hurt someone's feelings without regretting your own actions or putting yourself into a potentially volatile situation.

You can't control what the person is feeling or how they react, but you can try to understand it and sometimes an apology is helpful to diffuse the situation or even for safety. The stranger was practicing projective identification, which means unconsciously attributing our self-image or a feeling inside ourselves to someone else's assumed thoughts or feelings. In turn, they both hurt each other's feelings. It's difficult yet important to understand the emotional reactions—and their validity— of people who have different lived experiences from our own and to hold those experiences with empathy. Even if the other person reacts inappropriately, that doesn't change the fact that we upset them. Do your best to step outside of the abuser/victim dichotomy, as it does not allow access to empathy or realizing that you can inadvertently hurt someone's feelings.

There is also a big and important difference between hurting a stranger's feelings and those of someone that you love. When we hurt someone's feelings that we love, it's important to apologize but also not internalize the shame in moments when you didn't do anything wrong.

You can still be sorry to hurt someone even if it wasn't your intention. There's also a gendered dynamic in society where women (similarly to autistic people) are constantly pressured to apologize for other people's actions and feelings—things that really don't belong to them. Women and autistic people are often expected to apologize simply for existing because of patriarchal and neurophobic ideas in society. You can work through issues like this with your friends or partner on a micro level.

Your feelings are your own, but you don't have a right to other people's attention or body. You might feel angry to be rejected but this doesn't give you the right to these things. And similarly, even if someone hurts your feelings, you still don't have the right to their attention to process your feelings, just as you don't have to apologize for just existing. So in the example, it's possible to realize that you hurt someone's feelings without taking them on as your fault and still removing yourself from the situation.

Many of your dates and relationships—as well as family members and random strangers—will projectively identify their feelings to be the objective reality of any situation. Learn to comfort them, let it go, and don't argue once you figure out what is going on. If you are genuinely confused, ask what is going on. E.g. "You seem really upset and I don't understand. What's going on with you right now, can you help me understand?" will often get you a much clearer answer than telling them that they are "wrong." Or even asking "why?" Most humans don't respond well to "why" questions because the answer is... they don't know why. Or they feel a need to defend their response in a rational way. They are talking about their feelings, and feelings can't be wrong even if the information used to arrive at them is factually inaccurate or not acknowledging numerous important details.

FIGURE OUT THEIR BOUNDARIES

Just like yourself, everyone has boundaries. Remember, boundaries are the limits on how we allow ourselves to be treated to protect things that are yours—like your body, beliefs, choices, time, money, feelings, or investment—from being taken away from us without our consent. Think of someone's consent as an enthusiastic affirmative and boundaries as their politely declining something that doesn't interest them right now.

Just like yourself, other people have a right to determine how others get to treat them. This is usually done nonverbally through withdrawing or embracing a situation. Sometimes it's as subtle as hesitating or changing a facial expression. Again, while some people's instinct is to sustain continued pressure, it's much better to use clarifying communication. Something as simple as "I'm sorry. I'm having trouble understanding. Do you not want me to come over?"

While it can feel unwelcome or unpleasant to give someone the opportunity to pointedly and clearly decline what you want, it's far better in the long term. And honestly, how consent should work all the time. Selfishly hurting other people is bad enough, but by giving someone the opportunity to state their boundary, you are building trust that may change that answer in the future. You are showing that you respect them and aren't going to be pushy. What's acceptable to one person may be abhorrent to the next, so you don't want to make assumptions, lest you may hurt someone.

When I explained to a young autistic woman that I mentor that she has to respect the boundaries of her friends, she responded "My boundary is that I want to talk all the time and have him hug me and make him my boyfriend." Sadly, this is not how it works. That's a desire, not a boundary. We can cultivate hope for that relationship by showing that we are listening to their boundaries and respecting them. If someone has to repeatedly ask us to leave them alone, it defrays the relationship and slowly brings it to an end. I suggested instead that she not contact him whatsoever for three months and let him contact her when he wants to be in touch. She was *very* skeptical of this approach but I assured her that it would work. Sure enough, with enough distance he remembered what he enjoyed about her company and got back in touch. And if he hadn't? This is also OK, even if it's sad for awhile. When it comes down to it, someone is empirically not perfect for us if they don't feel the same way about us as we do about them. While this is a difficult concept for allistics to understand, neurodiverse people figure that out much faster once we put aside the narratives of books and movies and TV shows and all those allistic fantasies about romances and relationships.

An important boundary is personal space—the distance between two people. Think about personal space on a scale of 1-10, or if you are good at eyeballing measurements, you can think of it in terms of inches and feet, or centimeters and meters. Create a rule about how close that you stand to others. Observe how far away others variably stand from strangers, teachers, acquaintances, friends, and lovers. These distances change over time as culture and customs change so be mindful of that and continue to pay attention to others' distances, even after you think you've mastered this.

Dr. Faith took this a step further and cut pieces of string to help her oldest child measure a good distance between them and other people until they got better at approximating this on their own. Measuring appropriate distances between bodies communicates a lot to allistics about your intentions and how you see them, including your intent to date. For example, you would stand closer to someone that you are dating than to someone that you are interested in dating. But you'd stand closer to someone that you had intent to date than you would with a friend or a teacher.

The other reason for communicating clearly, asking for clarification, listening, and responding appropriately is that there are also cultural differences in how different people communicate, as well as in things like personal space. People, such as those from the south in the U.S., in an attempt to be polite, do not assert their needs. You may need to offer them tea three times before they accept. Turning you down the first two times is them being polite. This is terribly confusing because they aren't communicating honestly. Other people will reject your advances and offers in an effort to try to pressure you into giving chase. This is manipulative and fundamentally dishonest, so you don't want to reward it by giving them what they want. Remember, we are at risk of traps and being taken advantage of. Instead, by being straightforward, you can err on the safe side of trusting people and respecting their boundaries. If you find that someone is continually putting you in situations that don't feel good or safe, withdrawing will show them that they can't trick you into things as you try to respect their boundaries. Remember, you are in charge of your own choices as much as they are for theirs. And go back and remember your BIFF script when you need to communicate something, especially if the situation is tense.

Now that you have these basic building blocks, we're going to get into the specifics of various types of relationships.

FAMILY RELATIONSHIPS

In the previous edition of this book, we didn't even mention familial relationships. Perhaps we didn't want to go here because, even at their best, relationships with families are dreadfully complicated. Your family is different from romantic or platonic relationships, most notably, because of this societal rule: for your first eighteen years of life, and usually for as long as they are alive, no matter what you do, they won't abandon you completely and they will be loyal to you. This rule never made sense to me. My family treated me terribly for my entire childhood, were extremely violent, and did not leave me feeling loved through any metric of what a healthy nuclear family looks like. So I ran away as a teenager, eventually moved to Portland, OR, and built a new life here. I haven't really looked back. Decades later, I am occasionally in touch with the surviving members of my family on my own terms. They can't hurt me from this distance, which is largely the point, but many people judge me negatively for this decision. That's their prerogative. Their experiences with their family were different so they don't understand mine or my choices. Your choices are your own as well. One woman that I met at an Autistic Self Advocacy Network group told the story about how she learned social skills from joining a cult and living in close quarters after running away from her abusive parents. Your path is your own, despite what your parents will tell you. And almost no matter what it is, there will likely be some pain involved.

For most autistic people, our family is an unreliable support system and the source of our greatest pain. As such, your feelings around your own family are complicated and probably on a hair trigger at times. Mediator Lauren Gross explained to me, "I have a friend who told me once, 'Your family knows your buttons because they are the ones that installed them.'"

We're living through an era of history where *Saturday Night Live* offers humor about your racist uncle ruining Thanksgiving dinner. Given each person's filter bubble and the difficulty of obtaining information that contradicts their existing biases, it's important to understand where other people are coming from. Your family has a right to their own feelings and boundaries just like anyone else, and also has the responsibility of respecting your own. For most autistic people, our parents have a tendency to shelter us and try to keep us out of harm's way. Sheltering can be its own form of mistreatment because it doesn't result in us learning about the world or having enough space to make mistakes and learn from them. So feelings of frustration with situations that your family has put you in historically can linger for decades.

As you grow older, you will increasingly need to establish your own agency, the ability to make choices for your own life that are uniquely correct for you, even if your family doesn't agree. For most autistic people, you will outlive your parents, so creating a plan for as much independence as is reasonable at any given time is important. This is different on a case by case basis, but for the most part, the biggest trap that autistic people fall into is our parents either neglecting or smothering us, variously, at different times. So have these conversations about your wants, needs, and boundaries as conflicts come up.

Lauren Gross continues, "Chances are pretty good the same conflicts will come up again and again. More often than not, everyone wants to feel seen, heard, and validated/accepted for who they are. First understand how the other person is best able to hear and understand what they are being told. How do they like to communicate? Try to clearly communicate what you are needing and work on authentically listening and validating where they are coming from and work on validating their experience as well as asking for what you need. Non-authentic communication will be detrimental to getting anywhere and may harm the relationship further." Put yourself in their shoes. Consider the information that they have. Think about what their concerns are. Understanding their thinking is not agreeing with them or abandoning your own values. Instead of making accusations or generalizations about them, you don't need to have an argument. Think about your past investments in each other. If you have a disagreement, often empathizing with the other person can allow them to do the same or at least allow a conversation for two people who have different sources of information. It's OK to agree to disagree.

Relationships with your family are almost always different from relationships with your friends. While you may tell your family about a person that you are attracted to, an accomplishment, or an event that you are excited about, the relevant details are different. For example, you wouldn't share explicit details of a sexual experience with your family but you might share them with a close friend. This is because your friends are more likely to be at a similar development to yourself— meaning that you can relate about the same things being exciting. Whereas your family is more likely to focus on aspects that you don't know. If you went to a punk rock show in a bad neighborhood where people are shooting off fireworks and people are doing drugs, a friend might understand the excitement that you see in it. Whereas your family might only perceive the danger. Neither interpretation is wrong. Different people are at different points in development. This is why it's much easier to form meaningful experiences with someone who is a similar age and has a similar set of experiences to yourself.

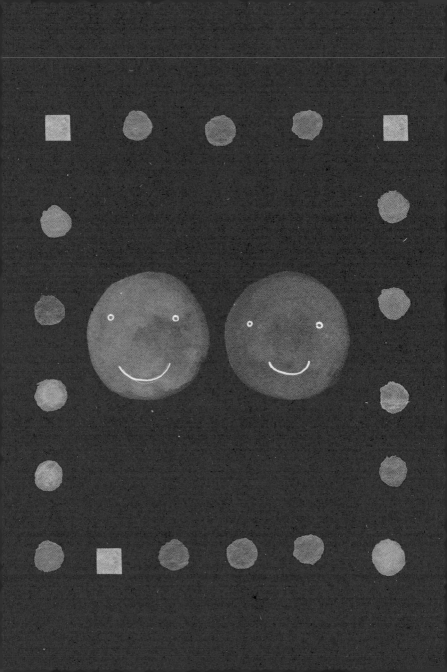

FRIENDSHIP

When I was a teenager I read about the depression plaguing toll booth operators and how the simple act of smiling at a stranger could literally change the endorphins in their brain, their mood, and their entire day. I could save a life! I thought "If it's this beneficial for toll booth operators, I'm going to do the world a favor and smile at everyone that I come across!" Of course in a world that is 98% allistic, this plan was doomed from that start. Most people assumed that I was flirting, had nefarious motives, or was buttering them up to ask for a favor. Women would tell me how uncomfortable strangers smiling at them could be and how they felt it meant they might even be the targets of violence. The world suddenly felt dreadfully complicated.

The difference between these reactions and friendship is that both the toll booth operator and people on the street are *strangers*. They don't know me and thus don't have a reason to trust me. The underlying assumptions of a stranger are usually to disengage, if not assume the worst. Whereas, in a friendship, the underlying assumptions are to trust your friend. So smiling at your friends can help them feel better. Smiling at a stranger may still reduce trust.

Friendship is the process of choosing to allow new people to relate with you and share experiences together. Unlike people chosen for you, such as teachers, coworkers, parents, or neighbors, friendships are relationships where you intentionally allow someone into your life to grow together. It's a mutual state of trust and support, like when two countries take care of each other instead of just looking out for themselves. We are stronger together.

You might choose to pursue friendships for all kinds of reasons. Some autistic people just want someone to play video games with while others prefer to do it alone. I don't really like playing video games, and that's a fine choice too. Some people pursue friendships to have someone that they can trust, relate with, rely upon, and confide in. Especially as unpredictable social dynamics emerge around you, it can help your self-reliance to not feel like you are totally alone. For everything from dealing with getting picked on to just reflecting on something weird or confusing that happened, it's nice to have friends. For yet others, friendships are a chance to learn and practice the skills of building a relationship that is uniquely your own, rather than a relationship that you inherited, like when your mom's sister marries someone and they come over for dinner.

So how do you make friends? Make your life attractive to yourself and the people that you want to be friends with and the right people will want to be your friend. Temple Grandin gives the advice that if you can become an expert in something, people will overlook anything that might have given them pause about your behavior previously. When I was a kid, my interest and expertise in everything from dinosaurs to Dungeons & Dragons to *Legend of Zelda* to punk music made me an attractive friend to people who shared those interests. As an adult, my knowledge, interest, and expertise in publishing, history, and autism create friendships with other people that are similarly fascinated in those areas. People love having "permission" to get really excited about stuff. Interest in these things isn't contrived to make friends. It's authentic so that your enthusiasm is genuine and you can relate and bond over these things.

Friendships begin by a combination of proximity, shared experiences, and common interests. You might find that you don't want to be close friends with the people from your childhood forever but the experiences of watching friends evolve will give you guidance for future decisions about who to let into your life as you get older. As you age, friendships become more focused on mutual respect than shared experiences, though there is always a mix of the two. Without shared experiences, the relationship is just looking up to each other. Without mutual respect, there is no emotional investment and the relationship is just someone that you know.

Autistic people tend to find it easier to be in proximity to other people in similar ways to how we spent time with our family of origin. We expect proximity alone to cause other people to feel that bond with us and for friendships to form. But without overt social activities together, this doesn't work. Other people tend to ignore us and form bonds with each other instead. When I was a kid I often found it easier to play video games alone in my room, even when my friends came over and wanted to hang out. They would do things in the yard while I'd be alone in my own head. I wanted to enjoy time with them but there were always extreme trade offs. I couldn't decipher their jokes or understand if teasing was meant to be fun or hurtful. If I teased back it was clear that I was going too far. It was easier to be alone. Very little changed in this regard in my 20s. I was most comfortable by myself, except by then I absolutely hated myself and felt so alone because I couldn't figure out how everyone else had such an easy time creating emotional bonds. Once, when playing cards at 22, a friend asked me what game I wanted to play and I non-sarcastically responded "solitaire."

When you are in proximity with someone that you want to become friends with, plan your time together to entertain both of you. If they hate sports, don't expect to watch sports on TV together. This shows that you either don't care about their experience or just don't want to be friends. If they like astrology, you could look at books about it together. If they like astronomy, you could go to an observatory together. Essentially, you want to build shared experiences that result in mutual investment. This will escalate your level of closeness.

If you are looking to make friends, get involved in stuff you are interested in doing anyway. Again, this is advice Faith gives to all of her clients. Volunteer for a cause you are passionate about. Join a biking club or yoga group. You will be in circles with other people who share your passion and even if you don't connect to new friend-people, it won't feel like wasted time and your motives aren't inauthentic.

Chosen family are the people in your life that you mutually select with your own free will to fulfill a similar point of deep emotional proximity—how an ideal biological family loves each other on television and always patches conflicts up at the end of every episode. Life is much easier with at least one or two people that you can trust and can be honest and open with without fear of judgment. For most people this is their parents or a different relative. I didn't have that privilege so I learned to find others in my life that I could come to for advice and trust their answers as reliable. I was not able to find people like this to function as my chosen family until my early 30s. In many ways your chosen family serves a similar function to what a biological family would for most people with happy childhoods. My current partner is the only person in my life that I've ever been able to trust 100% of the time and can go to when I need someone else's opinion about any subject. She has hurt my feelings sometimes—and I've hurt hers—but our trust and bonds are stronger than that. We can recover from these things together because we are so invested in each other. The function of your chosen family is someone in your life where you mutually trust each other to get their opinion about any situation. The function is much like your biological family, but they are select people who respect and understand you with greater compassion. They are people you celebrate holidays with, pick you up from the airport, and celebrate major life accomplishments together. This emotional proximity helps to unpack and understand others' motives and to know the difference between danger and someone that wants to form a relationship with you. Once you are invited to socialize, you must maintain constant attention to other people's experiences.

Autistic people take up a lot of space socially. We often lack awareness about the volume of our voice or how much of each conversation we spend talking, or how much of an emotional drain we can be on other people. For this reason it's important to put some rules in place. When you're in a group setting, even if it's just yourself and another person, divide the amount of time by the number of people present and try to talk *less* than that. Try not to talk for more than 30 seconds at a time unless you are answering a question or your expertise is sought on something that you know more about than others.

Instead of just smiling randomly (and apparently creepily), connect with other people in social situations by complimenting something that displays their personality, showing you are noticing things they *choose* over things they don't choose (namely, don't talk about their body). "Great t-shirt, I love The Cure!" is a much better conversation starter than "you have pretty eyes!"

Focus on being a nourishing friend: be friendly, tell funny stories to make people laugh, play to your strengths and use your uniqueness and differences to appeal to others, allow people to get to know the real you, practice as much emotional healing on yourself as you can muster, don't say more than one or two negative things in an entire conversation, give encouragement and compliments, act instead of reacting, and compliment others genuinely.

It's also important to understand that there are different kinds of friends. Each one has varying levels of emotional intimacy.

Casual friends are not the people that you put your deepest trust or secrets into. You serve a peripheral purpose in each other's lives and things rarely scratch the surface. We talk to them, they acknowledge us on the street, and we remember things about each other. These are your neighbors, people at work, classmates, or delivery people. You talk about non threatening things without a risk, like a cute dog that you saw or sports or the weather or current events without a sharp political bias. When a casual friend approaches you about a vulnerable subject, they may be initiating emotional proximity but they may also just have bad boundaries and not follow allistic rules (allistics are very forgiving of others who suffer from the *same* disability that they do but are less forgiving about other abilities). Evaluate if *you* want to escalate that friendship to become stronger and closer. If you do, engage with them and practice listening and empathy, understanding and sharing their feelings. Relate similar stories and experiences from your own life.

Casual friends become *close friends* through finding more personal things that you want to share with each other. Is there something that you value or respect about the other person? Maybe they are a great soccer player or a sharp dresser or really good at calculus or have a great collection of obscure conspiracy theory books or enjoy birdwatching in the park as much as you do. If you are interested in someone *only* because they have money, power, or nice things, these aren't strong points to bond over. That relationship cannot last because people in those positions are inherently leery of outsiders and being taken advantage of. It's important that you also genuinely enjoy aspects of this person's personality. If they also enjoy aspects of your personality, they will identify similar interests and traits in you to latch onto. Once you've identified a potential friend, you seal the deal by suggesting some activities that you can do together that simultaneously reinforce your mutual interests. "Want to compare Pokemon card collections?" or "There's a new *Batman* move that we could go see at the cineplex this weekend!" You don't want to overdo it by suggesting being best friends right away or offering an extended vacation together. Keep the stakes low and then continue to escalate as you continue to enjoy their company.

Even close friendship is a spectrum. Closest friends tell each other the most important, meaningful things going on in their lives. This is done by spending years together, getting comfortable, and enjoying each other's company. You can safely tell a close friend what makes you anxious, your biggest fears, or about a fight that you are having with your date. They might have advice or solutions but more likely they will offer sympathy, telling you about their own difficult relationship problems and consoling your pain. You can tell a close friend about your interests even if they don't share them. A close friend doesn't make fun of you. A close friend helps arbitrate complicated group dynamics or simply offers you an opportunity to escape a tense, hostile, or complicated situation.

A close friendship is not one-sided. It should have rules in place that benefit everyone fairly. Even if the rules are not equal, that's okay because different people have different needs and wants. But the rule should still be agreed upon by everyone. If unspoken rules start to appear, verbalize them and how they make you feel. For example, "every time that we socialize, we do what you want to do. How would you feel about doing what I want to do next time?" The biggest advantage of close friends is that they learn to recognize where you are struggling and thriving without you having to tell them or even recognize it yourself. In this way, their perspective is very valuable. They may know things about you before you do. A good friend accepts you as an autistic person and advocates for you, as well as helping you advocate for yourself. Sometimes someone looks, talks, and acts like a friend but when you think about it, their behavior isn't in service to you or the friendship. So it's important to think critically about this.

When you need help, ask a close friend. That is their role! The bigger the problem, the closer the friend needs to be. Sometimes asking for help with something that is too big for the friendship will bring you closer together but usually they will turn you down. For example, on the show *Parks and Recreation*, Tom Haverford's character invites his coworkers to help him move out of his house. They are already leery but do so out of social obligation. When they arrive, his apartment is not packed up, he displays no immediacy in getting ready, and after things are packed up, he only orders dinner for himself. This is shown to be funny but his actions demonstrate that he is selfish and doesn't want to strengthen the friendships with his co-workers. They are unlikely to help him again. Once, I ran into an acquaintance as I was leaving a show, she asked how I was doing and I responded that I was having a pretty hard time and needed someone to talk to. She looked at me funny and said "I hope that you run into a friend who can do that." She was politely asserting that our relationship wasn't at that point yet. It is twenty years later, and I'm lucky that I didn't burn that bridge by mistaking her greeting as a genuine request for information. It's important to assess the impact of your request on the other person and whether you think your relationship can sustain it.

The friendship dynamic is not easy. You need to be as reliable as you would expect someone else to be. If you make plans, follow through with them or cancel with as much notice as possible. I have often hurt my friends because my social skills were so unlike theirs that they misinterpreted my actions, words, or intentions. Once I hurt someone's feelings because I thought I was being pleasant and polite by making small talk when I ran into her in public. She interpreted my choice to make small talk as demoting our close friendship to a casual one. It took several weeks to repair this rift because she felt like we were close enough to only spend our time talking about "real" things. If you hurt someone's feelings, apologize for what you did that hurt them, and attempt for it not to happen again.

If weeks or months go by without seeing or talking to a close friend, that relationship will wither and fade away. You need to reignite and rebuild it if you value it. As you get older, friends will have more patience for this and will be happy to see you a few times per year and understand that you both have obligations besides each other.

Allistic people cannot read the emotions of autistic people. They say that we look angry when we feel calm and calm when we are in pain. If we don't make eye contact and take a long time to answer a question, allistics assume that we are hiding something or don't like them. This is yet another area of their disability that we must politely accept, and understand that they have limited ability to interpret our emotions unless we mimic the way that they express theirs. You may choose to do this or not. It's up to you. But your closest friends will accept you either way and will probably even be amused at your rants about the allistic disability. Shedding light on it is interesting, even if only because most people take it for granted.

Allistics also put an unhelpful layer of supposed meaning into everything. Like if we give them a flower, that doesn't communicate to them "you like flowers." Somehow it says "I have an emotional investment and possibly romantic interest in you." If you check your phone while they are talking, they assume you are bored or not invested in what they are saying.

As we age, the emotional development rift between autistic and allistic people deepens. From birth till about age twelve we are on an even playing field emotionally, with similar interests. But as allistic children enter their teens, their interests change as ours remain more childlike. That's when teasing worsens for missing social cues and not understanding things that come instinctively to allistic kids. It becomes more important to have close friends at this point in development as this is where social isolation pushes us into deepeningly worse mental health.

As autistic people grow up, our slower emotional development can be partially offset by the wider availability of peers our own age as a teen. If we live in a dense urban area, it's easier to make friends because we will find some people with similar development stages and interests, even if they are a little younger than we are. Fortunately, as we get older, we get more confident and thus it becomes easier to form relationships and make friends even as it becomes more difficult to meet people. By adulthood, allistics often perceive autistic people as immature, or worse, as hyper-intelligent, know-it-all adult children. This stigma is mostly because we express ourselves differently but also because of their own biases and social norms, what we think of as neurophobia. As a statistical minority that is also a social minority, you cannot singlehandedly dispel this prejudice on your own. You can, however, name behavior and do your best to use your superpower of not showing them that they hurt your feelings, even if it does. For example, if someone makes fun of your interests or clothes, it can be tempting to be defensive or insult them in return. Instead, develop a clever way of changing the trajectory and illuminating the situation, such as "I hope that picking on me at least makes you feel better."

Worse, allistics have a strange behavior where they perform modified or lite versions of themselves for various social situations, which is called "code-switching." Being able to blend in different worlds is a survival mechanism, like when autistic people mask. Just like making a crude joke isn't appropriate at a job interview, neurotypicals only reveal certain aspects of their interests or personalities with certain friends. This is somehow socially acceptable in their rule book and will be used against you when you do not practice it equally. You should make every effort to accommodate this disability. Showing only certain aspects of one's self is peculiar to autistic people since we are just inclined to be ourselves.

At my Autism Self Advocacy Network (ASAN) group, one regular attendee spoke in quotes from the TV show *M*A*S*H*, pointing at my service dog and asking "Were you a soldier?" I really enjoyed his company and perspective so I was quite surprised to hear that he truly preferred to be alone and that socializing at all for him was unwanted and unpleasant. He only came to the group because his therapist insisted that he must have some social contact.

You may be like the guy who speaks in *M*A*S*H* quotes and not crave human contact. That's okay and in many ways, lucky. However, even people that don't often enjoy interactions or feel strong connections to others can feel lonely. Social engagement is a complicated cocktail and withdrawal from it is usually a result of being repeatedly hurt or not understanding our peers. Typically, autistic people enjoy socializing but often we feel like it's not worth the risks. We tend to be mocked, bullied, and abused well into adulthood which makes us uncertain and scared socially to express ourselves. Do what you feel. Just don't hurt anybody as much as you can help it.

QUEER PLATONIC PARTNERSHIP

In Western society, the pervading mentality is that romantic relationships are emotionally *closer* or more *serious* than platonic relationships. Obviously, this isn't always true and it can be very harmful to think of romance as further along the continuum from friendship. All relationships are important and thinking in a continuum tends to result in our friends getting abandoned the minute we hitch up with a romantic partner. Conversely, this is why the exploitive and manipulative group, Pick Up Artists, refer to people who reject their romantic advances as "putting them in the friend zone."

As a result of this strange relationship dichotomy, queer people created the concept of the queer platonic partnership (QPP), which is a statement about the seriousness of the friendship without risking confusion that it's a romantic relationship or veering to become one. A QPP may involve certain agreements, like you might cuddle but never kiss. But fundamentally, the distinction is that you are close friends that are demonstrating your meaningful and emotional proximity to each other without being sexual.

This is important, if only to understand how limiting language and thinking can be around intimacy in most discourse. As an autistic person, it's easier to unpack the rules and social behavior around relationships because we have to do that around everything, but the ability to take the desirable aspects of all kinds of relationships and make an amalgamated version that suits ourselves and the people close to us is essential.

In reality, many people only share certain things with friends because their partner isn't interested in it or doesn't know how to talk about it. This is fine, as long as you aren't keeping hurtful secrets solely to "protect" someone's feelings (a boundaries violation). So it's okay to have a friend that is the only person that you talk to about serial killers but it's not okay if they are the only person that knows you are cheating on your partner.

Dr. Faith has a woman that she refers to as her "work wife." There are certain things that they can share that don't require the deep exposition to explain why something is frustrating or funny to her husband. They buy presents for each other to celebrate the relationship and demonstrate emotional investment, but she's not her actual wife or romantic partner (much to the disappointment of the internet). I have friends that also work in publishing whom I exchange text messages with all day long for the same reason. We send each other presents and can bond over success or hardship without nagging our romantic partners. We love these people and tell them as much. From the outside, these can be confusing because they look like romantic relationships but they are not.

Sometimes you'll find someone in your life that you have strong feelings for. It's a magical spark, but while you feel very close and this is confusing, your feelings are not sexual. You just find them easy to talk to and relate with. In these cases, talk about it. Creating a clear and established set of rules and expectations will lead to greater enjoyment for both of you. You don't have to model your relationships based on the ones on television but you do have to come to an agreement and understanding with those involved.

DATING

Romantic relationships begin by dating, which starts out as a loose agreement that two people are going to have some vaguely structured fun together. This is confusing because, at first and on the surface, it doesn't seem that different from friendship. Still, it's duplicitous to propose something as a friendship with the motives of transitioning that to romance. It's okay to keep things vague at first. Sometimes your feelings about someone will change as you get to know them, but it's absolutely vital to communicate your true intentions by the second or third occasion that you spend time alone together. Otherwise feelings get out of control and everyone becomes misled, scared, confused, hurt, or disappointed.

Fortunately for autistic people, dating is one area where everyone is lost, scared, excited, and confused. An allistic friend thought he was going on a date once to see a movie with a woman from school. At the end of the night she exclaimed "I'm so glad that I get to be friends with a gay guy." He isn't gay and this statement merely meant that he hadn't been overt enough that he was asking her on a date. She had mistaken his lisp and gender expression as his sexuality and assumed this to mean that there was no way they were on a date. If allistic people can screw up dating this badly, at least autistic people have relatively equal footing. And with sufficient understanding and preparation, we can excel.

GETTING STARTED

To get started on your path to dating, make a list of social activities that make you happy and that you enjoy. Just like with friendships, think of organizations and group activities where you can meet other people with interests and values similar to your own. These are successful brainstorms for meeting people as well as activities to do on your dates themselves. Clubs, classes, and volunteering within your interests is a great way to meet like-minded people. And you suddenly have something to talk about! As for what to do on a date, things like playing games, bike rides, playing with dogs, gardening, taking pictures, and watching movies are things that you can do with another person unobtrusively. Meaning, they are good ways to segue into a social life with someone without hours of forced, awkward conversation. Conversely, if your first date is going to dinner, you have to be social for an entire hour and that's a ton of pressure and opportunity for problems. You'll build up to that but start with an experience that you can simply enjoy. Together.

I joke that the best way to find a hot date is to stop looking for one. Suitors will flock to you everywhere that you go. This is because allistics interpret and process nonverbal communication and feelings differently than we do. They notice details—like confidence, when someone stares or ignores them, and how you interact with other people—that we don't and vice versa. And—as I've come to understand it in my allistic studies—confidence, hyperfocus, and intention are highly valued commodities. These attributes tend to make them look past other aspects of ourselves. Like if we are peculiar, obsessive, or even a hot mess. While hyperfocus and intention are something we excel at naturally, confidence needs to be worked on a bit. How do you feel confident? Channel the confidence of the most mediocre neurotypicals. If people with nothing notable about them can be so confident, look at the best attributes that you've got and what people have complimented you about in the past.

When I was in my 20s I had a friend named Sam who went on dates about four nights per week with different women. He was not extremely good looking. When I asked him what his secret was, he said that he was turned down about 95% of the time but he appeared to be so successful because he asked out every woman that he found himself in conversation with that he was attracted to. He's a bold individual and it's not exactly a model to mimic, but the point is that others' apparent success can be misleading.

So much of dating is building up your confidence based on small successes. When I was a kid our family of four was raised on $1,000 a month from government assistance. I wore homemade sweatpants with one pocket because there wasn't enough material for two. I was frequently mocked and bullied for my clothes, which were as nerdy as my interests. Fortunately, as I discovered punk rock in my teens, being schlubby and having ugly clothes was par for the course and by dumb luck the world decided that punk was again popularized in 1994. I already related with punk's energy, politics, and anger. By extension I became cool too. So to build confidence into adulthood I took that positive feedback and began to extend it gradually to create my own style. I became particular about colors and fashions and cuts of my clothes even if they still mostly came from thrift stores. This created a style. In 2014 I attended an industry trade show with over 30,000 people where a stranger came up to me and said "Wow! You're the best dressed person here!" I beamed. I was wearing a loud tie with dollar signs on it, a pink shirt, wingtips with orange soles like what you'd see on a running shoe, and a dynamic set of matching colors. It was a bold outfit and a risk for sure, so the positive feedback meant everything to me. I had become comfortable dressing myself and used that confidence to project bold moves in other areas of my life. Build yourself up from your small successes and turn them into larger ones, taking increasing amounts of risk as you develop more skills and confidence

Most flirtation is not communicated with words. It's expressed by the eyes, smile, or hands. Or just by being incredibly awkward and lingering around someone that you have a crush on. Pay attention to these things when people do it near you on a regular basis. Learn to look for those things. Have someone that you trust demonstrate what these signals look like. Make them yourself. Practice in advance. Similarly, practice your speech for asking someone on a date with a friend that you trust. Then practice having the kinds of conversations that will follow. Imagine yourself in the situation in advance, flirting with the specific person that you have a crush on.

It's okay to ask someone on a date even if you aren't sure that they are interested. Still, you shouldn't ask out people who are at work or on a bus because they have less power at that moment. They can't remove themselves from the situation if they feel uncomfortable. If you have never talked to the person that you are interested in dating, spend a few minutes making polite conversation first. Introduce yourself and compliment something interesting or attractive about their activities, apparent interests, or outfit, rather than something about their body. Asking questions about something they are wearing can be a good way to get them to open up and begin a little emotional investment. You can say "I love that band too! Did you see them on Friday?" or "Purple is great. Is it one of your favorite colors?" People want a relationship with someone who makes them feel happy, safe, and loved. If someone makes them feel that way, then they are often less concerned with that person's appearance, finances, or unique traits. So start off slow by making casual conversation without expecting anything.

Since women are frequently sexually harassed by allistic men, if you are interested in a woman, you have to perform a little bit of extra care to show that you have genuine interest in this person, and not just for her appearance. Women frequently have their appearance commented on in public, just as autistic people are often harassed and bullied in public. So go slow, be genuine, maintain some eye contact, and express your feelings. It's not fair that you have to go the extra mile because of how other people have treated her, but by doing so you put yourself in a higher tier by caring about her experience rather than just your own. Still, if she's not interested, you should accept that and withdraw yourself from the situation or at least allow her to.

No matter your gender and the gender of who you are asking out, it's okay to be disappointed if they say "no" but it's not okay to be shitty to them about it. If someone says "no thank you" a good response is along the lines of "fair enough, I had to at least take a shot! So anyway, seen anything good on Netflix lately?" It demonstrates good humor and a willingness to have a platonic connection with them. If you are only interested in dating them and not in friendship, just cut the final conversation shift sentence. Don't follow people around or persist if you are turned down. They might be dating someone else or not interested in dating anyone, or they might just not be interested in you that way.

Most people like to date people who match them socially and intellectually. It can be boring or alienating to attempt a conversation with someone that wants to drone on for hours about engines or bugs or a topic the other person has no knowledge about. Similarly, a person who comes from a certain amount of wealth is going to be most comfortable around someone else with a relatively similar amount of wealth, if only because they project the same coded cultural expression, like arranging forks on the table in a certain way. This has no bearing on things in the real world, but we are wired to be most comfortable around people who prioritize the same things we do.

While you can ask someone about their views or feelings about dating autistic people, the allistic disability frequently causes them to be dishonest so I wouldn't advise asking unless you feel very confident in the relationship already. Don't hold their lies against them (in this case). They may feel the need for safety based on prior experiences.

Do not attempt to date people considerably younger than you; especially if you are an adult and they are not. A good rule of thumb is to divide your age in half and add seven. That is the maximum acceptable age difference before it becomes too difficult to be equals and relate to each other. There are exceptions in emotional development but if there is a power differential between you and the other person, it is not something that you can turn into an equitable romantic relationship. For example, you should not date your family members, teachers, mentors, case workers, bosses, policemen, people significantly older than you, people in committed monogamous relationships with someone else, or anyone with a position of authority over you. In a relationship, both people should be relative equals and you don't want one person to have power over the other. If you are having sex in the relationship and there is a power differential, there is often undue pressure to do what the powerful person wants. Sexual pleasure affects your brain in fundamental, deeply emotional ways that can forever associate what would otherwise be positive experiences with traumatic, negative ones. Having a power differential complicates relationships and sex significantly. For some it's a turn on, which is fine (see the entire world of BDSM, which has even *more* rules!). But you need to be aware of it and everyone should be consenting when you participate in it.

If you are still nervous, confused, or embarrassed about dating, sometimes it's easier to send your questions in writing to people that you care about or someone who can help guide your understanding. These people can be older autistic people themselves or they can be people that believe in you and are invested in your personal success. Sometimes they are interested in understanding autism in practice. Someone that you trust for dating advice should be functional, independent, and thriving on their own. A struggling or damaged person is dealing with their own life and likely doesn't have time to help you with yours, but sometimes giving advice can help them build confidence. Either way, we need praise and support and someone who can recognize our strengths as well as our areas of struggle. This is important for several reasons, and how you respond is also important, as Andres Bravo expands on the allistic disability: "Allistics have a difficult time delivering critical feedback— even more so with the people they love. If their criticisms are negative, try not to be defensive. They have taken a risk to give you advice they genuinely believe will benefit your life. Much like exercising at the gym, just because it hurts doesn't mean it's bad for us."

For very understandable reasons, many autistic people prefer to date each other. It's easier. The shorthand is there. There's less to explain and it's not quite as much of a jump or a stretch as extending a toe into the 98% pool. You may have access to groups of autistic people but if you don't, this may prove difficult. Often you'll develop a crush or even an obsession on a singular person only to find that they don't feel the same way about you. You may find that your similarities end with autism. Many autistic people are asexual or simply find relationships too cumbersome to prioritize.

More and more people are using online dating apps as a means of meeting people. It is far and away the most common way non-heterosexual people meet each other, but they're catching up statistically as well. It gives you an idea of who is out there that you may not run into in your circles every day and who is interested in dating. This also allows you the opportunity to share about yourself and let others self-select out if they aren't interested. Keep in mind that certain dating apps have demonstrated drops in self-worth, especially for men, the swipey ones in particular (like Tinder and Bumble). They are intentionally set up to feel like a game which can be dehumanizing. It's something you really have to take with a grain of salt or take a pass on if you know that the inevitable rejections will feel personal.

When you find the right person that seems mutually interested in you, find a time when other people aren't crowded around you. Do not touch someone when you are asking them out. It's creepy and escalates the emotions of the situation. Most people respond very poorly to overt flirting because it's too much pressure. If you ask someone if they are married or dating someone in the first few minutes of a conversation, it reveals your motive and will likely alienate them. It also suggests that this person would be uninteresting to you if they were unavailable for mating, which is offensive and hurtful. For now, focus on creating experiences and memories together. Later you can recall them together or remember funny things that happened while you were talking that create a bond between you. Do not invite a date to your home or yourself to theirs as it implies sex, which is exciting and all, but this isn't the time for that.

Ask for a date in a clear and straightforward manner, e.g. "Do you want to go to a movie on Saturday?" If they turn you down, by saying something like "Sorry. I can't. I have to babysit my brother that night" you must accept that they are not available that day. If they seem interested but cannot commit to a date now, sometimes this is a "polite" way to say "no," part of the allistic disability. To test if they are declining without telling you or simply unavailable that one night, make an alternate proposal for a different activity or a different time. Respond with something like "Sure thing. Would you want to do something another evening or nah?"

If they say something like "Sure, that sounds fun," then you can ask "Maybe we could do something the following Friday?" If they still hedge, you can always say "Sounds like you're really busy, here's my number...text me when you know you're free if you feel like doing something." They may be trying to get out of saying no, and that stops the awkward suggesting of dates from here until next March. They might also turn you down indirectly by saying things like "Oh, my girlfriend and I are going to see some bands that night." Messages like that communicate many pieces of information that may be intentional to send you subtle cues.

If you set a plan, congrats! Even if you are excited, you want to keep your response brief like "Great, looking forward to it! We'll figure out the other details before then!" Try not to go overboard in celebrating in front of them. Save that for when you go home.

You may find that far too many people have very specific ideas and expectations of what their life will be like from a very young age and you don't fit into that. That's okay. There are other people out there. If you are turned down, take a moment to accept this person's perspective and make a list of reasons why they might feel that way. Don't assume it's your fault or that you are worthless because they aren't interested. Perhaps they want to be friends instead and that's a relationship that may be more satisfying. Accept their verdict gracefully, even if it hurts your feelings. It's far better to find someone else who is mutually interested in you than someone you obsess over who isn't interested. With persistence, you'll find wonderful specimens of humanity who love you in the way that you deserve.

Just because you've been rejected—even if it's often and substantial—does not mean that you have less worth or should accept just anybody into your life. Do not lower your standards. If you're having trouble, sometimes it's less intimidating for others to socialize in a larger group before going on a one-on-one date. If that goes well you could invite someone to a group setting where you are the only person that they know so that you two can increase your emotional bond and spend time getting to know each other.

ONCE YOU HAVE A DATE!

Once you are on a date, you do not have to impress the person. In fact, you should not try to. Be the version of yourself that you love. If you act out of character people will get the wrong impression or expect it all the time, and you'll have to continue the charade in perpetuity. You can acknowledge your faults and weaknesses if the topics arise but don't go out of your way to illuminate them. Instead, respond to things in your environment that are happening to both of you that you can remember later and form experiences around.

It's vital not to monologue over them the entire time. Ask about their interests, hobbies, and recent activities. Use this information to find common ground between their interests, hobbies, and activities and your own. If they recently spent time somewhere that you went on vacation once, that's something you can talk about together. It's important to remember that first dates are usually awkward, it's not your fault, and that it likely has nothing to do with autism.

If your date does something that you don't like but you like them otherwise, redirect their behavior. For example if they talk about something boring or that you don't like, change the subject to something mutually interesting. If they are trying to touch you in a way that is overwhelming, hold their hand instead. If they persist, state your boundary clearly and firmly. If they still persist, escalate one more time and if they aren't cooperative, end the date right there and then to establish your boundary. This will maintain your pride, show them that you don't allow yourself to be treated that way, and hopefully prevent them from attempting it again in the future.

On a date you can ask for clarification about unclear facial expressions. If you feel like kissing your date, you should ask if that's okay. You cannot force someone to touch, kiss, or have sex with you. Doing so will only end very badly for both of you. You will fundamentally hurt the other person in a way that you cannot fix and they will likely want nothing to do with you after that. Similarly, badgering someone over and over into doing something that they don't want to do is just as bad as forcing their hand.

It is necessary to ask before touching someone else. This rule has many parts. Some autistic people make the mistake of asking others if they can touch their breasts or penis in public places, like on the bus or inside a store. This is *never* okay. Even if both parties are consenting, it's upsetting for other people and could get you in trouble. Worse, asking this question in the first place imposes unwanted pressure. Touching someone in a sexual way in a public place where that behavior is never expected is unacceptable. The other person may feel the pressure to consent when they don't want to and you may hurt them. If you want to establish safer emotional proximity without going too fast, ask if you can hold their hand or brush an eyelash off their cheek. I once found myself dating someone from school that I found very attractive because they asked me to fix their hair one day. The more time that you spend together, the deeper your bonds will become and by waiting for sexual contact, it will be more exciting and it's more likely that the other person will be excited too!

As you pay attention to what your date says and does, you'll start to notice what makes them feel most appreciated. In his book *The Five Love Languages: How to Express Heartfelt Commitment to Your Mate*, Gary Chapman explains that there are different paths to different people's hearts. Chapman's views are deeply nestled in his religion, which can be enough to repulse some skeptics, but his core ideas are good. Chapman introduced the idea that some people experience love through doing things for each other, receiving gifts, quality time, saying nice things about each other, or physical touch. The premise, which is not scientific but is now generally accepted and effective, is that understanding what makes someone feel loved is far better than treating them like you want to be treated or what people respond well to in movies. I am much more receptive to someone bringing me special food than talking to me when I'm trying to focus on something else, for example.

You do not want to pry this information out of someone on a first date. But eventually it's an interesting and emotionally vulnerable topic of conversation, particularly if neither of you have a lot of dating experience. What makes you feel loved? You can draw on experiences with family and friends. What do you each appreciate? What do you not appreciate? Ultimately, these things are much more important than trying to perform the roles expected of you.

There is less precedent for social roles in same gender relationships. Society has less experience with these and as Andres Bravo puts it, "sometimes I don't know what is expected of me as a boyfriend. Who is expected to treat who to dinner? I've talked this over with my same gender partner, a cisgender man, and because his love language is receiving gifts I have volunteered to pay the bill on our dates. Bonus points for the masculine gender affirmation. Everyone wins when we explicitly state what we want, especially because I'm someone who thrives with direct and specific language." In these cases, talking it out and creating your own rules is best. Still, you can't prevent every conflict.

As you continue to go on dates, it's important to make sure there is enough room for another person (or two or three or more) in your life. Do not ever assume that your date will just want to accompany you for all activities in your life that you find enjoyable. They have their own interests, personality, and schedule. It's much more likely that you will be doing things that they enjoy instead at least half of the time, and perhaps enriching yourself in the process. Listening closely when they express themselves is important. If you think something important was said but you didn't understand it, ask for clarification, maybe even a few times.

If you are dating more than one person at a time, and are interested in polyamory in general, it's important to be upfront about that with everyone you are seeing. Once you go on a third or fourth date or two dates within one week, people expect to know the basic frame of your life. So it's important to tell them if you are dating other people. State this intention, even if it makes them uncomfortable. It's better to eliminate people that are not comfortable with this early on, or talk through their discomfort instead of bringing it up once they have feelings of investment in you. It's called consensual non-monogamy for a reason, and creating rules and boundaries with everyone involved is an important part of making multiple relationships work.

Relationships afford us personal growth, just like all people. Creating emotional proximity to others helps us to grow as people. However, dating cannot "fix" you. You have to be the active player in your life who proactively makes changes to become the person that you want to be. Resolving your old issues as you enter the dating field is an ideal time. You can decide to be the person that you want to be around someone new without the baggage of your past in that person's mind. This way you can actively attempt to shed maladaptive tendencies or coping mechanisms that weren't working for you. If you make changes like that years into the relationship, it will confuse and shock your partner. They may not be in a position to make similarly dramatic changes and it may distance you two. Oddly, dramatic personal growth almost always results in a breakup unless your partner is ready to go through a similar kind of growth at the same time.

STALKING

There are also a lot of things that you should not do. Refusing to take no for an answer, following someone around, or showing up at their home or work uninvited is called "stalking." It's scary, unethical, illegal, and something that you should never do under any circumstances.

The nature of autistic mannerisms often are confused for stalking by allistics because our behavior makes little sense to them, and because of projectively identifying our motives. Lots of TV shows and movies show people getting a girlfriend or boyfriend back through stalking behavior. Lloyd standing outside his girlfriend's window serenading her with his boombox in *Say Anything* is a classic example. In the music video for the Starting Line's "Best of Me," they take this a horrific step further where the band attempts to serenade the singer's girlfriend from her lawn. The lyrics are cringe-inducing. Which should tell you that in real life, you shouldn't do this. If someone says no and they don't *mean* no, that's on them. Not for you to interpret. Allistic people are learning this the hard way now that social movements are illuminating how many women are being harassed and assaulted by men imposing power over them. It's easier for neurodiverse people to understand "no" and get this message because it's the one that makes the most logical sense.

Perhaps due to my perceived vulnerability as an autistic person, I've been stalked numerous times in my life. The most notable was when I was a teenager. I worked at McDonald's and a co-worker there fell in love with me. I was already in a committed relationship with someone else and explained this to him. He didn't relent. He followed me home one night and began driving by my house regularly. When I got a new job he would routinely show up there on supposed business and feign surprise to find me there, making small talk. We were young and I don't think that he had any intent to harm me but there is no way to know that. Frequently, being obsessed with a person in this way leads to escalating behaviors until the situation is extremely out of hand. He didn't stop stalking me or apologize for several years, and I think he only saw the error in his behavior when mutual friends observed this and discussed it with him.

Faith has had similar experiences with people she dated deciding she was wrong for not wanting to see them and they were going to "fight for her" or they were going to challenge that she was "scared to be in an authentic relationship" when she just didn't want to go out with them again. Not just gross and presumptive but scary. Fortunately, her best friend is a big, hairy dude who is very good at threatening people who won't back off. If you don't have someone to scare away stalkers, the best thing that you can do is keep your distance, cover your tracks, watch your back, and wait for them to find a different target. At the advice of a crisis line, one person sent a specific email that said "do not contact me, do not come to my house, do not approach me in public, do not talk to my family" and that level of specificity stopped the behavior.

HOOKUP CULTURE

For some people, dating *is* about sex alone. This is called "hookup culture." You can find this on apps like Tinder or Grindr (primarily for gay men), where adults meet each other primarily for the purpose of sex, rather than developing a relationship. Done correctly, sex taps deep into the pleasure centers of the brain. Hookup culture, however, does not often result in long-term relationships. In fact, that is part of the point: that you aren't setting the expectation of an ongoing relationship, as opposed to apps like Bumble or Hinge, where you would go to find a relationship. This is helpful because you will not need to guess the other person's intentions and they won't have to guess yours. If you use an app like Tinder, you might need to decode who is interested in hooking up versus in dating with the potential for a long term relationship, and you'll need to state your intentions clearly. Andres Bravo warns, "In hookup culture, slang terms are always being invented and changed. Depending on the phrase, an invitation to watch TV shows and relax at home can actually be an invitation for sex. When in doubt, research the term online."

When negotiating sex with someone else, you will need to check in regularly about their boundaries as well as communicating your own. Things to talk about right away with any potential hookup include agreeing on safer sex practices, disclosing if either of you has an STI, and what specific actions and touch you each want and don't want. It's safest to meet hookups in a public place before going somewhere private for sex, so you can leave if you get a bad feeling about the situation or they haven't represented themselves or their intentions accurately.

Unless your mutual purpose is hooking up, never have sex on a first date. It does not allow the organic forming of emotional bonds between you and opens you up to continued pressure and regret. You may also find that you and/or your partner have no interest in sex. That's okay too. Go slowly and build bonds. The foundation of any relationship is mutual understanding, trust, and support. Sex is merely a form of intimacy and pleasure. Sometimes you will find that you enjoy each other as friends alone, despite the intention of sex or dating. And confusing as it may sound, all ongoing romantic relationships must contain a friendship as one aspect of your bond. Otherwise, the foundation will crumble because the elements of a relationship aren't there.

RELATIONSHIPS

As bonds form, sometimes two people become more serious and want to escalate from dating to a relationship. This is an agreement that you are both enjoying your time together and have mutual romantic interests in each other. Sometimes this means that you stop dating other people and date exclusively; sometimes it's a different kind of commitment. Once you've been dating for a while, it's important to have a conversation and establish exactly what your relationship is going to look like. You are both just saying that you feel that you are growing together emotionally and that your partner makes you a better person than you were before or would be on your own.

Autistic people often imitate the roles and characters that we see on television but it's really important to realize that dating and relationships are nothing like what is on television. Unlike other parts of life, stringent rules do not exist the same way in relationships. Establishing no rules around such an important area of human existence is a typical allistic disability. Allistics attempt to find gray areas between rules and exploit them to demonstrate the importance of their emotional narratives. But a relationship *can* and arguably *should* come with a set of rules in the form of boundaries.

Go back and refer to your earlier lists of needs, wants, and ideal schedule in a relationship, and update anything that has changed. Then discuss these issues individually with your partner. Your partner should present their needs, wants, and schedule as well. If they don't, this will create problems later so you should ask them to think about this and discuss with you. The sooner this form of discussion happens, the more likely it is to contribute to the longevity of your relationship.

Two people in a relationship become deeply invested in each other's emotional experience and life. If you cannot do this, you should not agree to it. Love is enjoying your time with someone else even if you don't feel the need to interact. You feel a connection with each other that is singular to that relationship. You can talk about problems and overcome difficult things together. You are not recreating a fairy tale so much as creating one.

When you've found a partner that you think you like, introduce them to your friends and people that you trust 100%. Get some opinions. Do they like your partner? What do they notice immediately about them? What do they notice about you two together? What are their concerns? Do they recognize warning signs that you cannot see? Love is complicated because our brain endorphins blind us from unpleasant details about our partner. Is your partner respectful towards you in private? In public? Are they considerate of your wants, needs, feelings?

An effective way to screen allistics is to ask them "What regrets do you have about your choices in previous relationships?" The reason that this test works is because allistics are so emotional that they cannot restrain themselves. So they might literally say "Nothing! She was crazy! I was a total *nice guy.*" Cases where one person is "crazy" and the other is a "nice guy"[8] are about one in a million. Faith can confirm this as a therapist. With all the couples she has worked with over the years, she can only think of one couple where one person was totally sane and great and their partner was 100% the problem. Everyone has *some* regrets about a previous relationship, even if it's just allowing someone into your life without proper screening. This question also builds trust because your partner admits mistakes and is vulnerable. You should offer similar personal information in return. It's appalling how effective this question is for causing people to self-incriminate.

If you are still unsure if you want to escalate to a relationship, try going on a trip together. See how you two handle the hurdles of dealing with

8 "Nice guy" is actually coded language adapted from *The Pickup Artist*, a book about how to trick women into dating men. It doesn't actually mean what it sounds like and it's often a way to be hurtful to others.

mild conflict and logistics as a team. Often the experience will bring you two closer or clarify what makes you incompatible. If so, fear not—one successful human proximity experiment means that you can find an even better date! If things are working out well and you don't have any misgivings, have the conversation about forming a relationship!

NEW RELATIONSHIPS

Congratulations! You're in a relationship! Despite your newfound success, it's important not to put too much pressure on your new partnership. Most people do not want their significant other to be dependent on them for happiness or try to make them act like a parent or dole out punishments. Your date will continue to be attracted to you because they see that you have a full life outside of the relationship. So continue to pursue your own meaning and purpose but make time in your schedule for your date so that they can see that you care about them too.

Once you are certain that you want to be in a committed relationship with this person and you have rules and expectations established, consider disclosing that you are autistic, if you haven't already. Remember, disclosure is important for two reasons: without understanding autism, people will pathologize you as a selfish asshole and you will have an opportunity to acknowledge how you perceive and interact with them. You slowly open the door about autism with each discussion about what your experience is like. And remember, hiding your autism undermines trust while disclosing builds trust. Your date probably won't be surprised and ultimately won't care too much about the label. They care about you and your lived experience and how society treats you. Ultimately someone that loves you will not think differently of you because of this. Together, you can build their acceptance and education and you can be better partners to each other.

When I was in a relationship twenty years ago, my partner read an article that I had written for a magazine about anarcho-syndicalist worker models and broke down in tears. She said that reading it showed her that she didn't know the first thing about me. "What do you want to know?" I asked. I didn't understand that she was asking to be let inside my emotional narrative. Communicating our inner experiences is difficult. I didn't know that I wasn't doing it and at that time I didn't see a point in doing it. We often struggle to express what comes naturally to allistics. Spend time understanding your feelings and emotional truth, and don't be afraid to talk to your partner about it. They may not agree with you, and that's okay. Either way, this will create trust. They will invest more in you as they get to know you.

At a trust building exercise when I was twelve, we went around a circle stating a fact about ourselves. After my third turn, the moderator interrupted to criticize me for not participating in the spirit of the exercise. He said "You know what you're doing." I had no idea what he was talking about because *I was cooperating*. The other issue is that I had been taught—through repeated bullying—that disclosing anything substantive about myself would only result in being hurt by people that I trusted. Like this moderator, your date wants to know more information than just your birthday, favorite color, and shoe size. They want to know your dreams, feelings, wishes, career goals, plans for children, what frustrates you and why, and what is exciting for you. Similarly, they want you to be interested in this same information about them. They want you to ask about this information and listen attentively. This is how they feel like you *know* each other; by knowing everything about each other. If you don't provide this information, they assume that you are withholding or repressing it because of distrust, a bad childhood, or being hurt in your past. When in reality, you just never thought to say it.

Remember, autistic people struggle with executive functioning—carrying from the idea stage to the goal. So often we are confused about how a series of decisions results in the outcome. Your partner can help you understand this and point out some things that you have missed, just like you can probably do for them as well. You should not offer this information about their choices without them requesting it or at least asking if they want to hear it first. If you need help understanding a situation or need coaching for major life decisions, a partner can be a tremendous asset.

LOVE VS DEPENDENCE

Love is seeing all aspects of the person that you are committed to, caring about each other, and encouraging each other to be your best selves without trying to change each other. In a relationship you should feel safe, trusted, mutually respected, and believe that there is a positive connection between you. For autistics, the payoff of bonding and emotional interaction is often lost because we don't see the intrinsic reward of emotionally sharing an interaction. It's one part having been gullibly bullied and one part just not seeing what we benefit from that encounter. But spending time doing this with someone that you trust will show you the value of emotional proximity with someone that you love.

Dependence is the state of relying upon someone or something in order to get our needs met. Sometimes this is depending on our parents to pay our bills, or for our lover to establish our self-worth, or only thinking you are cool because you have a cool friend. Dependence puts unreasonable pressure on people that we care about. It tends to result in many boundary violations as we try to make someone else protect our basic emotional needs. Dependence moves us away from learning skills of self-sufficiency. Being dependent requires twice as much emotional effort as being independent because it saps two people's energy. The dependent person puts their stock and self-image on how much they can bend the will and time of the other person. It's a lose-lose. Dependency motivates behavior that drives away the person that the dependent needs most. Until then, the dependent also will feel incapable of holding a boundary whenever they are asked to do something that they don't want to do. Does that mean you shouldn't allow a partner to support you? Of course not. But it should always be the two of you against the world, not them protecting you from the world all the time and keeping you propped up emotionally while getting nothing in return.

RELATIONSHIPPING RULES

I know that I said that there aren't rules for relationships but there are some important ones that never change:

- Don't tell other people things that your partner told you in confidence, or their secrets, like a medical diagnosis or something dramatic or intense that happened privately in their life. They trusted you with this stuff. It can be unclear or confusing sometimes so if you aren't sure if something is personal or a secret, double check. And similarly tell them what you don't want them to gossip around. This is generally true of all people and their secrets. If it isn't your story to tell then *don't*.

- Someone hitting you (or you hitting someone) is comparable to forcing someone to do something that they are not comfortable doing sexually; the outcomes, fear, and self-doubt are the same. This is domestic violence. Similarly, do not call your partner names or insult them. This is emotional abuse. These things never get you what you want, and only hurt the person that you care about most. You should never do them. They are major violations of basic human dignity that inappropriately cross boundaries and will leave your partner feeling nothing but resentment. There's a section at the end of this book about coercive control, if you want to learn more. One exception is if you practice BDSM and both parties consent to doing these things. This is also an exception to not having a power differential in the relationship. If both parties are aware of, comfortable with, and consenting to the power differential (or finding it hot) then it can be okay but there are even *more* rules for that! (see Dr. Faith's zine *BDSM FAQ* if you're intrigued).

• Your fears are not your partner's responsibility to overcome. They are yours. It may take therapy to move past them, and that's okay. You don't get to violate another human being's dignity because you're afraid of something.

• If you're ever *afraid* of your partner, that indicates a potentially very serious problem. Try to have a conversation about what is bothering you and assert the gravity of the situation. If they escalate instead of sympathizing, apologizing, or even listening, this is a serious red flag that something is very wrong. Get the perspective of someone that you trust to decide how to proceed.

• Your partner should not lie to you, be violent towards you in any way, or attempt to take advantage of you physically, sexually, emotionally, or financially. If someone treats you nicely at times and horribly at others, prevents you from having other friendships, or attempts to make you feel bad about yourself, this person is behaving abusively and you should terminate the relationship and seek help, such as counsel from friends, a trusted relative, or a therapist.

A relationship is figuring out the other person's feelings and honoring them. Often when there is conflict, we see everyone else's mistakes but cannot see how we contribute to these dynamics. Spend some time reflecting on things that you did that made a situation worse.

Some people choose to be in relationships with people who date lots of people. This is okay if it's part of your fundamental rules, though some people will certainly not approve of this. Autistic people need to be careful that this person is not lying to you or taking advantage of you. As always, the relationship needs to be mutual. You need to be able to express your boundaries and have them be respected.

For autistic people our tendency is often to accept the definitions, rules, and culture of others. But sometimes to create and feel emotional proximity we need to formulate our own needs, expectations, and wishes from a relationship. Meaning, we can't just repeat ideas of marriage or love that we saw in movies and expect that to be accepted by people that love us. We need to figure out how we *actually feel*. Make lists of your own wants and needs both for yourself and in a relationship. When you are having intense feelings, spend some time with them. Get comfortable and familiar with them. Feelings are just information, often quite important and vital. Use that information to understand what you want and need.

LONG-TERM RELATIONSHIPS

For me, going grocery shopping is just about the worst daily horror. The lights are punishing. The place is gigantic and confusing. Just as soon as I figure out where to find things, they are moved to new locations. Then I find that what I want is out of stock. Strangers want to talk to me but they don't want to listen to my responses. I'm always in someone's way. Children cry because they cannot pet my service dog. Their parents demand that I just let their kids play with my dog. Fortunately, my loving partner understands how painful this is for me and handles the grocery shopping for our family. Similarly, visiting the doctor is often a traumatic and appalling experience for me. Bringing my partner with me often makes that much easier. Or at least someone else can witness the horror. These are some material benefits of a long-term relationship: being emotionally understood and someone responding to those needs to make your life better.

A relationship isn't a one-way street. For my partner, I manage our shared social calendar, manage our household, build cool shit that we need, fix things that are broken, and code spreadsheets to help her understand things that she can use to better understand patterns and trajectories. This is what *our* give and take looks like. Operating as the same team instead of one of us being overly dependent. I listen to her problems empathically and offer support without trying to solve them. If we have a disagreement or see an issue in different ways, we talk about it and find a collaboration that doesn't compromise either of our experiences.

Of course, before my diagnosis we clashed and didn't understand why. When I had a particular financial windfall, I wanted to make a major purchase that would support both of us. When my partner couldn't understand how I was going to afford it, I responded "Don't worry your pretty little head." I had probably heard this saying on television as a child. I did not understand the connotations of this phrase, since when it was used on television it had elicited a positive response. In hindsight, television is a terrible place to understand acceptable social behavior but at the time I wasn't thinking critically.

My partner was horrified. The connotation was that she was not smart enough to understand the finances at play. I thought that I was calling her pretty and telling her that I was taking care of things but I was actually insulting her and keeping her in the dark about a very important decision that we should have been making together. We talked about it over the next few weeks and I came to understand why she was upset and she came to understand the logistics of the situation.

These negotiations do not always go so well. In a different long-term relationship, my date insisted that I wake them up every morning at 8AM like an alarm clock. This interrupted my schedule and seemed unnecessary, so it annoyed me. But it annoyed them more because my motions to wake them were robotic when they wanted a warm interaction. One morning this escalated to conflict and I was told that I needed to "learn how to be a better friend." I took out my pocket notebook and made a note to "learn how to be a better friend," repeating the phrase in monotone as I wrote. My date, increasingly irritated, demanded "don't you see how annoying your behavior is?" I didn't.

For a few months as a teenager, I dated someone a few years older than me who worked part time in a bar. I made considerably more money. About two weeks into our relationship, we went past a restaurant and she, somewhat jokingly, demanded that I buy her dinner. We were heading back to her house, where she, an adult, was already going to eat dinner. So I declined... perhaps too dismissively. For the remainder of our relationship, she called me "selfish." This confused me *because I knew what selfishness was.* It's a lack of concern for others. Demanding that I buy dinner for her at a time when it was neither necessary or practical; when there was no implicit need at all, was not a product of my supposed selfishness. It was a logical product of my problem-solving mind, because I didn't understand that her love language was probably "gifts" and me taking her out made her feel special and cared for. But that was the judgment that she placed on me and harped about it endlessly. It was an emotional narrative that overwrote a logical one. And I didn't deal with either of them in a way that allowed for healing. Similarly, I criticized just about everyone that I dated for their inability to budget their money, not realizing this was both unwanted and unhelpful. Criticizing them wasn't helping them to learn. It was shaming them for not knowing something that is honestly pretty complicated.

The other problem in both of these cases was that we treated each like "fixer uppers." We saw each others' faults but expected that they would go away rather than accepting them or dealing with them together. Behaving in these ways are horrible recipes for failure. We need to accept our partners how they are, and where they are at. We cannot expect them to fix themselves up *for* us, let alone in the way that we expect or demand. Sure, these attempted relationships were trying to "make each other into a better person" but, condescension besides, growth has to be on our own, individualistic terms based on what we want and need out of life. A person can fix themselves for the sake of maintaining the relationship, but fundamentally, they must want to fix themselves *for themselves.*

LIVING TOGETHER

Eventually, in the course of a long term relationship, two partners will usually want to live together. When you cohabitate with your partner, you need to divide tasks. This conversation can be confusing for allistics because they tend to think in terms of equality instead of equity. As Oboi Reed of Slow Roll Chicago explains, "Equality is making sure that everyone has shoes. Equity is making sure that everyone has *shoes that fit*." In a neurologically mixed relationship, this means that different tasks affect different people in different ways. My partner is horrified by rodent corpses, so it's my job to remove them from the house and dispose of them because it doesn't bother me. As mentioned above, grocery shopping has a disproportionate toll on me and normally leaves me in bed for the rest of the day. I am strongly affected by stimulus and smells and social interaction. These things do not negatively affect her in the same way. For whatever reason, emptying the dishwasher invokes every traumatic memory from the depths of my brain. I try to do it anyway, because it's painful for her to feel like she has to clean up after me. As such, I must make a concerted effort to put away trash and dishes as soon as I am finished with them. There were years in our relationship where I was bedridden from lead poisoning and an inability to turn food into energy. Essentially, I couldn't contribute to household chores so when I recovered I tried to do as much as I could. There are still traumatic memories for both of us from that time, so it's important not to invoke them. I try to take out the trash, clean the kitchen, and load the dishwasher each morning because I wake up first.

We find that we both often hold onto assumptions about the other's motivation and ability to perform various household chores and it benefits us to have conversations about things that would normally seem unnecessary. At one point, a decade into our relationship, my morning tea leaves in the sink were really upsetting her and she was resenting me for it. What we each considered the logical and obvious solution did not work for the other person. We solved the problem easily by discussing it and hearing where each other was coming from. While it might seem unnecessary, talking about household labor for five minutes per month and coming to agreements will save years of painful arguments. Faith would say, once again, this is true of all relationships. Neither she nor her husband are neurodiverse, but still have struggled with mis-reads on household tasks and the like and she has learned over the years that while he has zero problem sweeping and mopping the floor he will absolutely not notice that this task needs to happen. She could resent that he is Captain Oblivious or she could ask him to tackle the floors while she's picking up the groceries.

It is likely that you and your partner might each have different standards of cleanliness. Discuss them. When I was in my twenties my eyesight was so poor that I could not see how dirty the house was, which was a great comfort for me—other than being constantly chastised for the conditions that I found acceptable. A friend was happy to wash all of the dishes in his home, but he is blind so his partner would just have to wash them all again. It was a sweet gesture, but it wasn't helpful and his efforts were better spent with other chores.

If having a clean and tidy home is important to your partner, create an order of priorities for chores, such as childcare, pet care, removing garbage, organizing, bathroom cleaning, kitchen chores, managing clothes, paying bills, cleaning floors, shopping, self-care, dusting, furniture maintenance, and seasonal duties. Organizational tasks can be very difficult for autistic people, including sorting things into piles. We have a more difficult time because we perceive so much more information and memories about each item so it's more difficult to focus on what is relevant for this exercise. For example, bills and nostalgic keepsakes can both be paper, but go in different places because they serve different functions. The better that things are sorted, the easier it is to find them when you need them. Sometimes an organizational system that works for one person doesn't work for another. Most people describe my desk as "a mess" but I can find exactly what I need in two seconds without getting out of my chair. But this doesn't work for other people as my systems make no sense to them and they are nervous to leave papers in my inbox, for fear that they will get lost. In an ideal world, I would just leave my clothes on the floor and take the things I need out of the pockets the next day. My partner and I have each made compromises in our household to find a system that works for everyone. I am allowed to keep as many glass jars as I want, as long as I can fit them in a cabinet. She drew the line that I was not allowed to maintain a library of television sets in front of our house, suggesting instead that I print stickers to place on television sets that other people are giving away. Decide who is doing what and determine what are daily, weekly, monthly, and annual activities. Figure out a day each week to catch up on neglected tasks and don't try to do things on days when you have too many activities already.

My best practice rule is that if something takes less than five minutes and I have the energy, I do it immediately. If I lack the energy, I put it on a list which I sequence based on what is a priority or urgent. This ensures that the important things are getting done instead of the things that I think of first. You will find that the more that you do, the easier it becomes to do more. By challenging yourself a little each day, you can increase your overall capacity. But if you get overwhelmed, never forget to ask for help. Keeping lists and visual reminders in plain sight where you can find them (on the fridge, by the front door) can really help set your mind at ease and jog your memory about things that are important to you.

Similarly, you will want to create rules about chores, guests, noise, messes, gatherings, decorations, food, pets, and how time spent together will change once living together. I always leave my keys and clothes in the same place so that I can find them the next morning when I need them. But depositing them on the floor as soon as I entered the house wasn't acceptable to my partner so we collaborated. If I am well enough, I disrobe in the bedroom. If my clothes are found on the living room floor, she understands that this is a product of my condition or exhaustion.

You will reach a point where you are a packrat for no real reason other than habit. Your date will likely not approve of or appreciate this. If you don't need something anymore, get it out of your house. By "not need," I mean if it's not sentimental and you haven't touched it in 18 months, put it outside to get rid of it. If it is sentimental, but you haven't looked at it in three to five years, get rid of it unless you are an archivist or it's *extremely* sentimental, like childhood photos. Some things you might need later, but if you keep everything you won't be able to find what you need when you need it, simply because you'll run out of organizational space. While it can feel like defeat, it's often better to risk replacing something than to hold onto everything. Every year I purge my hardware and book collection. I could use door hinges in the future but if I haven't touched them in a year, odds are that I won't. If a book makes me happy or I might read it again or loan it to someone, that's a good reason to keep it. If looking at it is frustrating, that's a good reason to get rid of it. I have a shelf of books that I have borrowed from other people. I should really see about returning those. Autistic people can be very excited about the particulars of recycling and trash disposal. We have someone at work who loves to memorize the exact science of how best to dispose of things.

Break every task into manageable pieces so it's not overwhelming. At first, just do an hour of household work each day. If things are *really* bad, focus on a single square foot until it's perfect then move on to the next square foot to your right. Over time, learn to keep certain spots clean all the time and always place certain items in them, like your phone, keys, clothes for the next day, and wallet. Then you will never have to look for these things when it's time to go somewhere.

As the relationship advances, pay attention to what makes your date feel loved. Remember the five love languages? Do they like random, thoughtful gifts? Intellectual praise? Making them coffee in bed every morning? Having snacks available in your bag at all times? Doing the dishes and vacuuming every weekend? If you are unclear, ask them what makes them feel loved. They may not know yet but if you pose the question they can think about it and get back to you. Often we put our efforts into programmed activities rather than what our date actually appreciates and makes them feel loved. Most people make the mistake of doing for our partner what we like or things we have seen be effective elsewhere instead of what they like. By having a conversation you'll prevent yourself from resenting them for not appreciating your effort and they'll love and appreciate you even more.

Most importantly, when you succeed and finish something difficult for you, reward yourself. Don't stop in the middle of the task to give yourself a reward. That rewards the wrong behavior. If you reward yourself when you finish or achieve a certain milestone, that informs your brain doubly that you are a champion!

SEX

Sex is a big part of most people's lives and romantic relationships. But maybe you don't even want that, and that's okay too. Still, most people will expect that, so even then it's good to at least understand it and sometimes it can be pleasuring to pleasure someone you love. At least on occasion. It's not the foundation of a long term partnership, but it *is* that super-important spray insulation foam that fills in all the cracks and gaps, keeping the foundation airtight. Sex is generally an instrumental part of connection and communication between partners.

One important thing in a long term relationship is negotiating how to be intimate together; what each partner likes physically. This is confusing at first because the cultural monolith dictates that touch and pleasure are instinctual and universal as modeled in pornography. In reality, porn is not representative of what sex is like in real life. What one person likes isn't the same as another, and we often lack the most fundamental knowledge about our own likes and dislikes in this department. Similarly, you might find that what you thought would feel really good for you was actually pretty disappointing, either because of cultural expectations or how your partner behaved. Just like actually having sex, sometimes it can be very awkward, painful, and difficult to have a conversation about sex. Autistic people tend to have unique experiences around sex and tend to talk about it in the superlative. Either "the most overwhelming thing I've ever experienced" or "that was the most unpleasant thing I've ever had done to me" or "The best/worst communication and experience I've had with my partner." This is because of our 400% resting brain activity. We experience more stuff, including during sex. If you are interested in sex, this can be managed and Dr. Faith has created some great exercises for couples to get to the bottom of this. If you want more, check out her books *Unfuck Your Intimacy* and its accompanying *Workbook*.

If you aren't yet dating someone seriously, it's still a good idea to really spend some time thinking about what you like and what is of interest or even physically pleasurable. This way you'll be prepared when you discuss these things with future partners. If you're unsure what you like, you can check out Dr. Faith's *Sexing Yourself.* Knowing what feels good to you will make that conversation much less stressful and confusing when you are having it.

SENSATE TOUCH EXERCISE

Sensate touch exercises (also called sensate focus exercises) were developed by Masters and Johnson to help couples work through intimacy issues. They are very helpful in rebuilding partner intimacy regardless of what caused the problem to begin with. All forms of touch are important in our romantic partnerships and all help foster a sense of intimacy, and these exercises were designed to build on all four of these levels. One of the most important ways of doing that is not only improving our communication about touch, but also finding true enjoyment in both giving and receiving touch from our partners.

One of the biggest barriers to fostering intimate touch, both sexual and non-sexual, is the expectation of return demonstration. Instead, the giver should focus on the pleasure experienced in touching their partner, rather than focusing on what they get when it is "their turn." All relationships have a give and take, but except for the first pre-touch exercise here, time always should be set aside for the receiver to enjoy the experience without being expected to return the favor. Giving pleasure for its own sake to your partner can be its own intensely rewarding experience that fosters intimacy in and of itself.

Modify these exercises in *any* way that you need. The goal is to make *you* comfortable.

Goals of the Exercises

- To learn how we like to be touched.
- To learn how our partner likes to be touched.
- To find new ways to explore our needs and desires.
- To find new ways of receiving and giving pleasure without focusing on immediate sexual release.
- To demonstrate to ourselves and our partner a commitment to our relationship.
- To help build connection and deepen our relationship with our partner.
- To become more comfortable with our physical selves as our bodies evolve and change through childbirth, aging, and/or disability.

Establish Ground Rules

Before you begin, it's a good idea to discuss what you hope to accomplish. It's a good idea to establish some boundaries up front:

- Determine if there are any areas that you do not want to have touched, and how you will communicate if that changes during the exercises. Consider a safe word or gesture if you are concerned that you may struggle with communicating your needs.

- Decide ahead of time if you desire to be clothed, partially clothed, or naked during the earlier stage sensate touch exercises.

- Consider how you will handle any unexpected outcomes. For example, one partner or both may become sexually aroused and want to engage in more than sensate touch. There is no rule, of course, that you cannot engage in activities other than sensate touch during your touch sessions, however neither partner should feel pressured to do so. Having a plan on how to handle those issues ahead of time will help prevent hurt feelings or unfulfilled expectations.

Afterwards, talk about your experiences and whether or not you think the goals you set at the beginning are being achieved. Discuss the positives and negatives of each encounter. Use "I" statements to demonstrate your own accountability for your thoughts and feelings.

How to Do the Exercises

Once you've talked over your goals and boundaries, pick a time and place where you will feel comfortable and won't be interrupted by other people or by the telephone, TV, or other intrusions. For the sensate focus exercises, consider doing them in the morning if a male partner is the receiver, as testosterone levels are highest in the morning. Use lighting that feels comfortable to you and music if you find that soothing. If you aren't using your bed for the initial exercises (which makes sense if that's become a source of pressure), you can still use plenty of pillows and blankets to feel comfortable wherever you are.

Use lotions, oils, or a powder for the massage exercises (make sure to use one that is face friendly for the face caress, like a moisturizing cream). Some people find lotions and oils to be slimy and prefer talc or cornstarch (which doesn't clump, is economical, and is probably already in your pantry). For the exercises that include genital stimulation, you may want to use a lubricant. This can be especially helpful if one of the partners has issues producing enough lubrication due to menopause or other medical conditions or struggles to maintain a full erection. If you have not used lubricant before, read all the labels and test it out on a small area on your skin to make sure you do not have an allergic reaction. Remember not to use oil-based lubrication when using condoms or silicone-based lubricants when using silicone-based toys.

Alternate being the giver and the receiver. You can take turns during the same occasion or set separate times so the receiver can fully enjoy the experience, without having to return the favor after they are relaxed.

The person receiving the touch should state what feels good and what does not. Communicate this using "I" statements. "I like it when…" and "I don't like…" rather than "You shouldn't…" or "Stop that!" Positive redirection such as "I prefer…" always feels best to the giving partner. Positive feedback in general is always preferred, especially noises of appreciation when your partner does something you especially enjoy!

The giver should ask for feedback about areas of touch, pressure, and technique. One way to learn what the receiver likes is letting them guide your hand, especially at first. Consider using your non-dominant hand for times when a lighter touch is preferred. For autistic people, a firmer touch is normally preferable as a soft touch can be overwhelming. But since this is a time for experimentation, see what feels good *to you*. As you notice your partner's response to receiving certain types of stimulation, take time to focus on the sensations you feel as the giver. What does your partner's skin feel like? What does the part of your body touching them feel like as you move over their skin?

There is no time limit or limit to the number of sessions you spend on any exercise or stage. You can spend as much time as you want on each exercise before moving to the next one in order to establish comfort and trust. It is important that partners do not pressure each other to move forward until both are ready to do so. It can be very helpful to spend several weeks on a particular stage and exercise, incorporating a bit more of the body or areas of the body each time you practice.

Remember, the aim of these exercises is enjoyment, relaxation, connectedness, and pleasure. Focus on the journey rather than the end result.

Pre-Touch Shared Breathing Exercise

Sit facing each other. Maintaining eye contact, slow your breathing and focus on breathing in unison. If you don't have medical issues that disrupt your breathing patterns, try to breathe in to the count of three, hold for the count of three, and release your breath for a count of three. Focus your thoughts on loving intent toward your partner, such as "I choose you" or "I care for you."

Continue this pattern for two minutes. Two minutes will seem like a very long time the first time you try this! You can continue these exercises over time, extending the amount of time you spend in shared breathing.

Discuss the experience with your partner. What did you notice? Did anything make you uncomfortable? Was there anything you particularly enjoyed?

The Hand Caress

Sit in a comfortable position, facing each other. Using a lotion, oil, or powder gently rub your partner's hand. Spend 5-10 minutes on each hand (10-20 minutes total). Explore each finger, the pads of their fingers, the lines of their palms. Check in with your partner about the amount of pressure you are using. Focus your thoughts on loving intent toward your partner such as "I choose you" or "I care for you."

Discuss the experience with your partner. What did you notice? Did anything make you uncomfortable? Was there anything you particularly enjoyed?

The Face Caress

Pick a position that is most comfortable for you. Many people find it works best if the giver is sitting and the receiver is lying flat on their back with their head resting on the giver's thighs. The giver should first rub a facial-friendly lubricant, like a moisturizing lotion, or powder like cornstarch on their hands. Begin with the chin, then stroke the cheeks, temples, and forehead. Check in with your partner about the amount of pressure that you are using. Explore your partner's earlobes, and the indentation just behind the earlobes on the neck. Return to massaging the temples. This exercise should take about 10-20 minutes. Focus your thoughts on loving intent toward your partner such as "I choose you" or "I care for you."

Discuss the experience with your partner. What did you notice? Did anything make you uncomfortable? Was there anything you particularly enjoyed?

Sensate Body Work
You may have noticed that the first exercises were more in the healing and possibly sensual domain. This is where we start to move into erotic and sexual!

Stage One
Limit touching and stroking to areas of the body that are not sexually stimulating. Start with areas that feel safe for your partner and incorporate more areas on future turns. Oftentimes, individuals have the first session lying on their back, being touched only on the front of their body, where they can see everything their partner is doing. If that feels comfortable, start a later session with the receiver laying on their stomach and having you work on their neck, shoulders, back, and backs of arms and legs.

You can continue to include the hands and face, but also include feet, legs, and arms. Be careful for areas that are ticklish. Continue to focus your thoughts on loving intent toward your partner such as "I choose you" or "I care for you."

Discuss the experience with your partner. What did you notice? Did anything make you uncomfortable? Was there anything you particularly enjoyed?

Stage Two

Start with the touch you used in the first stage before moving on. During the second stage, you can include genital areas in the places you touch and stroke, but the intent at this point is not sexual arousal but sensual response.

Often during stage two, individuals find it works best to start by incorporating touch of the breasts and nipples, then touching areas around the genitals. Oral touching as well as manual touching can be introduced here (or in later stages) if both partners are comfortable with it, such as light kissing, licking, or sucking.

Continue to focus your thoughts on loving intent toward your partner such as "I choose you" or "I care for you."

Discuss the experience with your partner. What did you notice? Did anything make you uncomfortable? Was there anything you particularly enjoyed?

Stage Three

Start with the touch you used in the first two stages before moving to the third. During the third stage, include touch of the genitals with intention to arouse. If they have a vulva, stroke the clitoris and/or gently probe the vaginal opening with a finger. If they have a penis, stroke the shaft and the head (including the frenulum, which is the spot where the head and the shaft of the penis join). This can include stroking the anus if the receiving partner has expressed a desire for you to do so.

Continue to focus your thoughts on loving intent toward your partner such as "I choose you" or "I care for you."

Discuss the experience with your partner. What did you notice? Did anything make you uncomfortable? Was there anything you particularly enjoyed?

Stage Four

Start with the touch you used in the first three stages before moving to the fourth. And, as with the other stages, not doing this one at all is completely fine. If penetrative intercourse, however, is something you want to include in your sex life, stage four is designed to get you there.

During the fourth stage, you can attempt vaginal or anal penetration either with a finger, penis or sexual aid, depending on your partner's preference. The extent of penetration and what you use for penetration and where you experience penetration is entirely up to you. For example, people who experience vaginismus (an involuntary contraction of the muscles around the opening of the vagina) may need to start with a q-tip or a small vaginal dilator before even a finger is a tenable option.

Continue to focus your thoughts on loving intent toward your partner such as "I choose you" or "I care for you."

Discuss the experience with your partner. What did you notice? Did anything make you uncomfortable? Was there anything you particularly enjoyed?

These are exercises you can continue using or go back to regularly as you find them helpful.

It may feel hokey, but the more time that you spend with exercises like this, the more comfortable and bonded you become together. Sex becomes a time of intimate sharing. This way you get a much better idea of what is pleasant before the pressure of performing physical intimacy is upon you.

HEALTHY CONFLICT VS ABUSE

In all kinds of relationships, you'll have conflicts, disagreements, and arguments. Occasional conflict is normal and not a sign that the relationship is broken or ending, though it might feel like that in the moment. If you and your friend, date, or partner treat each other with respect and trust, and listen, or are at least able to calm down and work out a rational compromise later, conflict can make your relationship stronger. These rules are the same for any kind of relationship—intimate partners, friends, coworkers, or even strangers.

Unfortunately, not all conflict is healthy, and telling the difference between a healthy, spirited argument and manipulation or control can be difficult to spot, especially for autistics. So we are going to work on some skills for healthy disagreement and avoiding either abusing the person you are in conflict with or being abused.

When I was a small child I brought one of my favorite toys to a friend's house. We played with it all day and had a great time. Eventually my mom came to pick me up and when I left, the friend demanded that I leave the toy. My mom explained that it was my toy and that I was taking it with me. The other kid began screaming and crying and proceeded to chase us out into the snow as we got into the car. Confused, I asked my mom why they were saying that I had stolen the toy. Did they not remember that it was my toy? She explained that it was my toy but they were really upset. "Shouldn't I leave the toy then?" I asked. Getting irritated with me, she said "No, it's yours and you don't always give away something that is yours just to please someone else."

This is good advice but it was extremely confusing to my six-year-old autistic brain, and it took me another 30 years to internalize the lesson. This kid was trying to emotionally manipulate me. Through screaming, crying, and demanding that I do what they want, they were trying to influence my behavior in order to do what was in their best interest but not in mine. Similarly, I would often trade my toys for broken toys with neighborhood kids. While they were trying to take advantage of me, I didn't mind because the broken toys captivated my imagination just as well as the other toys.

As a teen or adult, the stakes of manipulation are much higher. Sadly, 80% of autistic people will suffer sexual violence or abuse in our lifetimes, most likely at the hands of someone that we know. Those wounds run deep and take decades to truly get past. Even when we know what is safe and what is not, we still end up being harmed. We are taken advantage of by teachers, priests, bosses, co-workers, "friends," and partners. Autistic people have a hard time perceiving when people are lying to us. Worse, somehow allistics can sense that autistic people are vulnerable. I've run into nefarious allistics attempting to exploit me and concerned ones who assume that I cannot take care of myself when I want to be left alone. Autistic people tend to be trusting and our rigid rules for thinking can put us in harm's way, because we cannot always see duplicitous motives, or see a dangerous situation before it is enveloping us.

Sometimes we find ourselves in a social situation that is not abusive or manipulative but the other person's behavior is still upsetting. Take some time to sort out your feelings before responding or acting on them. Also, make sure you are not doing this behavior yourself. You cannot "make" someone else do something. To attempt to do so is manipulative. State your needs and wants and if someone is doing something that makes you uncomfortable, say so. Do not accuse someone of not caring about you because they won't do what you want. You will soon find yourself alone. Similarly, you cannot make someone feel jealous. Statements like "If you loved me, you would do this" are false and exploitative. Instead, learn to negotiate and collaborate. When people care about you genuinely and know how to get their own needs met, you'll find that they are inclined to work things out in a way that suits everyone.

Humans have a tendency to fall into patterns of shame where we internalize our hurtful behavior as a part of ourselves and see it as inevitable. It's important to understand the difference between regret and shame. In the former, we see hurtful behavior as an isolated incident and a mistake rather than as a part of ourselves. In the latter, we internalize our worst behavior as inevitable and embrace it, allowing our self-esteem to slip lower and lower. Just because you have hurt someone's feelings does not mean that you are someone who hurts people's feelings. It means that it happened in certain incidents. Your worst mistakes or behaviors do not define your character. Repeat that to yourself regularly.

When you sink into a pit of despair like this, it's not reasonable to ask your friends to deal with your problems as a replacement for professionals. If you need a therapist, hire one. Don't try to force a friend into the same role. Your friends can console you and make you feel better but they cannot undo trauma and it's not fair to expect this from them. However, your friends can help you to understand patterns and values that you hold dear as well as things that you might not have realized about yourself. This is called "wise compassion" as opposed to "idiot compassion," where a friend directs you away from your behavior patterns and assures you that this is not your fault. Part of the trick here is that you have to ask for this and show that you want this information and will be receptive to it. A good script to try is "I got fired from another job today. Do you think that I'm doing something that causes this to keep happening?" And then you have to actively listen instead of reacting. If you yell at your friends for providing vital information about your personality to you, they will stop doing it. If you thank them and offer a thoughtful and lively conversation, the interaction will grow your relationship and cement mutual trust. If strangers seem to offer wise compassion, you should usually disregard it as they do not have enough of a sample of your patterned behavior to draw from and are largely speaking about their own perspectives and biases, rather than anything about you. Even feedback from people that are close to you may not feel accurate to you but if you keep finding yourself in the same situation, consider what consistent thinking and behavior that you are employing and could change.

You can bring your friends' wise compassion insights and revelations to therapy. If a painful event happened in the past 90 days—like you didn't get a job that you were really excited about or your date dumped you—talking about it with a friend is a helpful way to cope and move on. If the trauma is bigger—a lifetime of abuse from your parents, or an ex that continues to stalk and harass you fifteen years after the relationship ended—it's appropriate to tell your closest friends about it, but you will need to work through the issues in therapy.

Friends have other roles too. When I had terrible migraines and the doctors couldn't help me, it was a friend who explained that a certain weed growing in my yard would relax the blood vessels in my brain, which got rid of the migraines. Another friend thought it was foolish to trust a peer instead of a doctor, but I am more inclined towards the helpful person in this scenario. Indeed, my friend was able to solve in a few minutes what the doctors had failed to for years.

Someone that I thought was my friend told me that I was not autistic because I had friends. He had taught autistic kids for the past decade and had first introduced me to autism. I presumed he introduced this topic of conversation because he thought that I was autistic and we certainly joked about me being autistic and having the symptoms and behaviors. When I was formally diagnosed six years later I expected him to understand the nuances a bit better. After some difficult conversations, it became clear that he works with children and did not understand how autism manifests in adults. I felt like he was denying my experience as an autistic person, so I demoted him from a close friend to an acquaintance. I clearly couldn't trust him with my feelings or even my reality, and I've been happier not to continue having to justify such a central part of my character and personality. Since then I've been fortunate to make new friends and they can see and accept my autism, even if they don't know very much about it. I've certainly been in tense conversations with other friends who told me that I'm not autistic because I have emotions or other neurophobic ideas, but, fortunately, we were able to talk through their misconceptions and lack of knowledge about what autism is. These conversations, even when painful and tense, tend to make two friends closer. I strongly feel that when we have the chance to educate others about our lived experience of those of marginalized people like us, it is not our responsibility but it is an opportunity to make the world a better place for the next person like us that they interact with. Having a moment with someone who trusts us and is receptive to learning new information is rare and the opportunity should be seized.

Remember, autistic people tend to struggle with executive function. This is often a source of our conflict. Repeating behaviors that haven't worked is unlikely to work now. A neurodiverse person at work was tired of having things disappearing from common areas so they left a pair of scissors, a marker, and a boxcutter on everyone's individual desk. But the problem wasn't lack of access—it was immediate proximity. When you need a marker or boxcutter, you look for the closest one. You don't go back to your desk. So when the problem continued, it was a source of confusion and frustration for everyone.

Similarly, in one ASAN group, I met several people with multiple masters degrees who had never had a job. They were told that college degrees would get you a job but that wasn't working so they kept trying it. I've met autistic people who volunteer with social service agencies thinking that they will be recognized and get a job that way. Autistic people have a way of trusting when we shouldn't. In one case, an autistic person that I knew went to the county employment agency every day and wondered why they couldn't place him in a job. He repeated the same actions over and over and wondered why they didn't have a new outcome. On one hand, these are exploitative aspects of capitalism for other people to benefit from us. On the other hand, it's a matter of being unclear with our intentions and using critical thinking to find patterns.

You shouldn't tell someone that you want to just be friends when you want to be lovers. You risk that they might take you at your word, which they should. My partner jokes that my existence is upsetting to people with a narrow worldview because I am so good at learning the rules and exploiting the gray area between them. This approach may not suit you, but the important thing is to look critically at the amalgamated outcome of your actions.

Sometimes friends gravitate away from each other; even when we don't want them to. Sometimes we have less in common with each other over a period of years. Sometimes we develop different interests or social circles. Sometimes it's mysterious why someone is no longer interested in being our friend or even that fact is just not clear to us. Sometimes we make the choices no longer to be friends with someone as well. That's healthy personal growth. Perhaps our needs changed and that person is no longer meeting them. This can feel bad but ultimately it's a fundamental part of personal evolution.

If you keep going back to a friend after each resolved conflict, assess if you are getting anything out of the relationship or you are acting out of habit or desperation. What do you need from them? What can you reasonably get from them? As counselor and astrologist Jessica

Lanyadoo explains, "Don't process with people that you don't trust." If someone is unreliable, why trust them with your feelings? Talk to someone else about it. Instead of blaming others or stewing on your anger, deal with your own responsibilities, shame, and things that are within your locus of control. Your friends will see that, respect it, and respond accordingly.

COERCIVE CONTROL

Abuse is a serious issue in all kinds of relationships—families, friendships, work relationships, romantic partnerships—but it's not always easy to identify, so we're going to talk about it in its most harmful form. Coercive control is a form of abuse that is almost always legal and involves the strategic application of boundary violations as a means of controlling another human being. It refers to regular patterns of boundary violating behaviors that create fear-based compliance in someone. The term was coined by Evan Stark, whose 2007 book has the same name. His work brought to light how another person's systemic, organized boundary violations create an ongoing pattern of behavior that takes away our freedom of choice and ability to define our own personhood.

Dr. Stark's research shows that coercive control is present in up to 80% of abusive relationships. Which means only 20% of abusive relationships are defined purely by physical violence. Because it isn't something that is measured effectively (when it is measured at all), it is impossible to guess the number of relationships within the general population in which one partner abuses the other through these patterns of coercion.

Coercive control is strategic, rational, and ongoing. It's not reactive in the heat of the moment. Individuals who engage in coercive control are seeking the measurable material and social benefits they can achieve by shattering the psyche of another person in order to own them.

And because mind-games, degradation, isolation, intimidation, regulation, and an ever-changing "rule book" are not illegal actions, they are even more effective at holding another human being hostage than inflicting physical pain. It's not the physical abuse, it's the mind-fuck. It's emotional terrorism. And it's the real reason it's so hard to leave an abusive partner. And the reason that so many abuse survivors suffer from PTSD.

Once physical and sexual intimate partner violence started to become socially unacceptable in the 1970s, individuals who abuse had to find other ways to maintain control over their victims… the uptick in coercive control in the past few decades correlates strongly with an uptick in legal consequences for perpetrating physical and sexual harm on a partner.

Dr. Stark notes that coercive control is steeped in gender-based privilege (and in case you are wondering, he is a cis/het dude), therefore the focus of his work was on cisgender, heterosexual relationships in which male partners used coercive control techniques against their female partners. He notes that women are more vulnerable to coercive control because of their unequal political and economic status which allows cis men to systematically take advantage at greater levels. Which means we are seeing how insidiously *normal* rape culture is.

The numbers in this regard don't lie, but in Faith's experience as a therapist, she can absolutely attest to how coercive control extends beyond this narrow definition.. Coercive control exists within all manner of intimate relationships, in LGBTQ+ communities, among family members, within friendship groups, and within employer-employee relationships.

Remember when we talked about how important it is for people in relationships to be on equal footing? This is one reason why. The common denominator of *unequal status* still applies to the dynamic of controller and controlled. Those with less power are far more susceptible to oppressive behavior by others whom they rely on for food, shelter, financial support, and/or safety.

How do these dynamics get created? It's a systematic, conscious process. Living in a society that centers power-over dynamics allows and even encourages means of owning the bodies and spirits of others. While most of us do not engage in that level of abusive power, there are plenty of people who do. There is a predisposition component (nature) to being a coercive controller, but it is far more a learned behavior (nurture). When people realize that they can perpetuate this kind of harm over another without consequence, they continue to do so.

A controlling individual sets the stage by cutting off their victim's means of support from the beginning. They seek out individuals who have vulnerabilities they can exploit, such as autistic people. This may be people who are marginalized in significant ways (being poor, undocumented, isolated, etc.) or people who have the kind of abuse histories that have created permeable boundaries that the controlling individual can subvert almost immediately.

The coercive controller sets themselves up to become a rescuer in some fashion and creates an indebtedness in their disempowered victim. They may rescue them financially from a bad situation. Or love bomb them with showered attention and care when they are at a low point and desperate for affection. They tether the vulnerable partner by ensuring more and more attachments to them and fewer attachments to others. At this point, resistance is worn down instead of strong-armed away.

If you recognize yourself living these patterns, do know that there is support for getting out of an abusive situation. Even if they have never hurt you physically, domestic violence agencies can help you strategize a plan to leave safely (or stay safely, if that is your best option currently). There is a list of warning behaviors to look for after this section.

Is Coercive Control a "Fixable" Thing?

Most people who set out to control others don't want to change; in these cases, it's much more important to focus on the safety of the victim. But that's not the case universally. Research demonstrates that when individuals experience therapeutic support that focuses on establishing equality and appropriate boundaries in relationships, along with behavioral strategies to manage violence and systematic desire to control, they can stop treating other people this way for good.

In fact, research shows that this type of support works better than incarceration for preventing future violence. Which makes total sense: the prison system is generally designed to perpetuate power-over models and reward power-over ways of thinking. The model developed by Ellen Pence in Minnesota, the *Domestic Abuse Intervention Project*, has demonstrated high success rates and is now used across the country. There are also therapists who do this work in solo practice. You can search for offender treatment providers in your area, or call your rape crisis center and ask for clinician referrals.

And *yes*. Faith has worked with individuals who saw these red flags in themselves and wanted to unpack the histories that led them to this behavior, so they could make different and better choices in the future. And Faith has seen them go on to have healthy relationships. We can't go back and change our pasts, but we can make a conscious decision to say this behavior stops *here* and *now*, and make significant changes.

The big indicator of success in changing abusive behavior was that the coercively controlling individual had self-awareness of what they were doing and *wanted* to make that change. So if you see these red flags in your own behavior and are realizing that you *want* to change? That level of introspection is bad-ass. If this is work that you are looking to start in your own life, the exercises in the *Unfuck Your Boundaries Workbook* and *How to Be Accountable* are a good start... but you will likely need support in making some serious changes in your relationships. But having healthy, fear-free relationships in the future will be well worth the effort.

AUTISM AND ABUSE

Like Christopher Knight, the neurodiverse person who lived without human contact for 27 years in wooded Maine by robbing unattended cabins, I once planned to live alone on a desert island. It seemed like the only way to prevent myself from hurting others' feelings. The allistic world is so confusing and it's difficult to see that *everyone* hurts other people's feelings. Meeting people that respect my boundaries allowed me to have healthy relationships that continue to this day. And I came to realize that I had allowed others to hurt *my* feelings, just accepting that this had happened and even taking it for granted.

Because of neurophobia and misunderstandings about how empathy works, autistic people are frequently misunderstood to be sociopaths. While autistic people have trouble understanding the emotional states of others, sociopaths have no trouble with this and use that knowledge to exploit those feelings and insecurities. Allistics see us hurting others' feelings and assume that we don't care or take joy in doing so. Remember the two different kinds of empathy? Once we can connect others' feelings to our own, we care *more* than allistics do but this does not stop people from maliciously hurting us in response. And as Jessica Lanyadoo says, there's a weird idea floating around that it's okay to hurt people when we feel like they have been hurtful. People who are perceived as disabled are able to be dehumanized. It's probably best not to think too much about why. Point being, we have feelings and it's not okay to intentionally hurt anyone.

Life before and after diagnosis is very confusing, and we suffer a lot of trauma without understanding what is an acceptable way for ourselves to be treated. This almost always results in heightened anxiety and depression which begin to mask our symptoms of autism, further confusing people about what is going on internally for us.

Remember the two different kinds of empathy? Affective empathy is the instinctive ability to experience others' emotions while cognitive empathy is the conscious drive to recognize someone else's emotional state from their speech, behavior, and nonverbal communication. A sociopath often has a low level of affective empathy and a high level of cognitive empathy, meaning that they know what is the correct response and how to exploit it without actually experiencing it. An autistic person tends to have the opposite configuration: a low level of cognitive ability to recognize others' experience but an extreme, visceral reaction to it when we understand what's going on.

Autistic people can abuse others, but in reality, we are more likely to be the victim. Coercive controllers and sociopaths are rather adept at detecting our vulnerability without experiencing our emotions, which process as an error in the code or nothing at all to most allistics. And autistic people's reverse wiring of empathy—not able to read others but experiencing it deeply—prevents sociopaths—or even nefarious individuals—from setting off our radar. We want to trust. They want our trust. We rely on direct communication. They use this information to mislead us.

Most of your encounters will not be with sociopaths or coercive controllers and the interactions will be much more rote and harmless. Still, allistics tend to get frustrated with us, even when they don't pathologize us to be sociopaths. Once I was in a relationship with someone who would get very angry that I could not read her mind, know her feelings, and interpret her body language. We once tried dancing together and after two minutes she just stared at me and said "I feel nothing." I didn't either but I didn't know what I was supposed to feel or what she expected. I felt like this was a huge failing in myself. Within two years there was a fundamental lack of trust in the relationship, causing both of us to disclose less and less to each other about our inner lives. Relationships in this state almost never recover, but if you deal with the little things before they become dire, you can rebuild trust. Relationships of all kinds require intent, cooperation, and effort from both parties, and probably a couple's counselor too. You regain trust through understanding and empathy. And if you cannot trust each other, that's basically impossible.

Nowadays I understand my shortcomings and try to account for them by choosing my activities and the people that I allow into my life more carefully. I disclose as is safe and appropriate. And I find that the more empathy I have the less annoying other people are. At one point my doctor told me simply to practice compassion for all people, myself included. It's a good exercise. Perhaps as a result of all of this, I met my current partner of over ten years who is willing to meet me in the middle, between each of our instinctive behaviors and interpretations of the world.

But even under the best circumstances, you're likely going to run into some nasty situations. Like being taken advantage of socially and sexually. I have been numerous times and, while I'm not proud of it, I've learned a lot from these situations. You're most likely to be put in a situation like this by someone that you already know, whether that's someone that you went on a few dates with or someone that is related to you or that you've been in an extensive relationship with. White men are statistically the most likely to be violent towards you but almost every kind of person struggles with maladaptive coping and abusive behaviors that might lead them to mistreat you.

If you are ever in an unsafe situation, in that moment, do whatever you need to be safe. Sometimes that includes things that would normally be unacceptable like hitting, screaming, running away, biting, or kicking. You may want to consider taking a self-defense class, no matter what your gender is. And if it's legal to do so where you live, carry a taser and pepper spray (Dr. Faith does, for what it's worth). You will also need to work through the trauma by journaling, talking it out, or in therapy—ideally during the first 90 days afterward—so that it's not forever sitting in your subconscious scaring you out of an otherwise wonderful life. Otherwise you will continue to feel anxiety, depression, guilt, shame, eating problems, trouble sleeping, addiction, and problems in your other relationships.

Several autistic people that I talked to thought that they had "cheated" on their partner when they were sexually assaulted. They all felt shame, like they had brought these attacks on themselves. If this happens to you, it's not your fault. You were taken advantage of and attacked. This happens to all kinds of people. One person, who managed not to internalize the attack, cooperated with a rape because they cognitively knew it would be less likely that their attacker would murder them afterwards. Let's hope that nothing like this ever happens to you but if it does, use it as an experience to learn from and take the time to heal your trauma.

OVERCOMING RELATIONSHIP TRAUMA

When you experience a traumatic situation, the steps towards healing are:

• Talking to someone that you trust about it so it's not just in your head

• Work through all feelings that you have about the situation so you do not blame yourself. Someone else can see these experiences more objectively than you can

- Forgive yourself for choices that put you in that vulnerable situation

- Be angry at the person who hurt you

- Forgive the person that hurt you so that they no longer hold power over you. Right now you are chaining yourself to them and you need to break that chain so you can move on without them. Just because you've forgiven someone does not mean that you should let them back into your life.

For example, my whole family was beaten by my mom from the time that I was a small child. I eventually escaped the situation as a teenager and it took years to really experience all of the emotions. Most people didn't want to hear about it or would find ways to justify her behavior. Eventually, I processed it all in therapy and stopped being angry at her. I didn't want her to have that control over me. And at 80 years old, she finally apologized for treating me this way. I still didn't feel any need to let her back into my life. I wasn't sure that I could trust her and I had long ago moved on. But I still appreciated the apology.

Most importantly, my strongest advice to all autistics is not to internalize the pathology that we are sociopaths or garbage. I am of the strong belief that nobody is a "garbage person" besides the people who pick up your garbage (and those are good jobs). When someone criticizes you in this way or paints you with broad generalizations, take a cold, hard look at their complaints. Apologize for hurting them. Own the parts of their criticism that you feel apply to you and move on with your life. It's like being caught with your pants down. If you get embarrassed and spend the rest of the day talking about it to everyone, you'll never get anything else done. If you zip it up right away and move on with your life, you can learn from that and before long it's like it never happened.

There are therapists out there that work with neurodiverse people, and if you are looking for a therapist to help you process past traumatic occurrences, you should ask what their experience and training is with neurodiversity. If they can't give you a thoughtful and positive answer, keep looking!

THE "NO" TEST

Violence and abuse aren't overt in the beginning. They often start with a sense of ownership that moves into coercive control and, sometimes, external boundary violations. So even if you are in the throes of Something New(™) and things are pretty great, it's a good idea to see how New Person responds to boundaries.

The No Test is the brainchild of Australian domestic abuse counselor Rob Andrew, and it's amazingly simple. It is simply an evaluation of how someone responds to being told "no" for the first time.

It's far better to do this early on, and with smaller issues, before you're married and fighting over whether or not to baptize your children.

Example: When Mr. and Dr. Faith had been dating about a month, she had to attend a work holiday party. She mentioned going, and he said he would be happy to attend with her. When she responded with a *"No, thank you,"* he understood immediately and said, *"Too soon? I respect that."* Well played, Woke Bae.

You are looking for signs of control in their response. Someone being disappointed at being told no is totally normal. Someone being irritated or agitated at you not going along with their plan is a sign of a controlling personality. Do they argue the point? Do they try to force a "yes" rather than negotiate around your expectations?

The No Test can be an important part of the healing process for individuals who have been victims. It's about recognizing and prioritizing your boundaries over the comfort of others. Once you truly internalize your right to say no, you are far less likely to take responsibility for someone else's response to your boundary.

SIGNS OF A COERCIVELY CONTROLLING PERSON

When listed on paper, these activities seem pretty obvious, but when you are living this experience they sneak up in such a manner that we don't always see it until we step back. This list is based on the items used by researchers to measure coercive control in romantic partnerships:

- Controls/limits your contact with others (friends, family members, etc.) for instance by phone, internet, or chat.

- Wants all your passwords and access to all your accounts (but you don't have access to theirs)

- Tracks your movements through your cell phone (for your "safety")

- Makes demands regarding your movements (where you go, when you go, who you go with)

- Has physically stopped you from going somewhere or leaving the house (doesn't have to be by laying hands on you—they could block your exit, hide your keys, etc.)

- Spies on you/stalks you to check in on your movements

- Checks your clothes/receipts/items in the home for signs of your activities

- Audio or video tapes you either without your consent or by threatening you into consenting.

- Asks others about your activities (your children, family members, friends, neighbors)

- Makes demands about your appearance (that you look or dress a certain way for them, or maintain a certain weight)

- Controls household resources (bank accounts, vehicles, use of jointly produced income)

- Controls access to medical care
- Demands sexual intimacy in general, or specific sexual acts (either with them or with others on their demand)
- Controls use of contraceptives or STI prevention methods
- Interferes with or threatens your immigration/citizenship status
- Creates other legal trouble for you
- Threatens your housing stability (e.g., threatening to kick you out of a home they pay for, breaking rules set in a home rental to have your lease terminated and get you both evicted)
- Controls all parenting decisions and parenting tasks
- Threatens harm
- Displays physical violence towards others or property to frighten you (punching walls, hurting a family pet)
- Otherwise scares you into submission
- Threatens self-harm in retaliation for your behaviors
- Engages in self-harm in retaliation for your behaviors
- Keeps you from work/makes you late to work/disrupts your workday/gets you fired
- Destroys your property
- Destroys the property of your friends and family
- Keeps weapons and makes threats (overt or veiled) to use them against you or someone else

RED FLAGS OF A MANIPULATIVE PARTNER OR EARLY STAGE COERCIVELY CONTROLLING PARTNER

Along with the above, more overt behaviors, there are a lot of practices that also serve to wield power over another human being. These could be early warning sign behaviors in a new relationship that may become more intense as time goes on, or they could be occurring in longer-term relationships indicating a problem with systemic boundary violations. These behaviors are more belittling than controlling, but when done in a systematic way can invoke the process of wearing down resistance we see in coercively controlling relationships.

- Rude or dismissive of your friends and family
- Does not want you doing things with friends or family without their presence
- Excuses all their behavior rather than accepting accountability
- Needs constant contact with you through the day
- Engages in behaviors outside your value system and expects you to excuse them as "no big deal" or "jokes" (such as racial comments)
- "Jokes" about your appearance, passions, intelligence, culture, gender, or identity
- Challenges your worldview, motives, etc consistently (rather than asking to better understand them)
- Otherwise does not support your values and passions
- Picks fights so you feel obligated to make things up to them
- Always expects you to wait for their attention, doesn't value your time
- Never admits any fault in past relationships ending
- Expects you to be okay with their behavior when it's not okay for you to engage in same said behavior
- Is rude to people they see as beneath them (service workers, waitstaff)
- Minimizes your feelings and dismisses how their choices and behaviors affect you in negative ways (such as accusing you of being too sensitive)

- Frames your disagreement as you not understanding or listening to them effectively
- Questions your judgement ("Oh, you're wearing that?")
- Challenges or belittles your decisions, even decisions with little consequence
- Threatens you with social embarrassment
- Disrupts the well-being of other people in your life in order to disrupt your well-being (your children, family members, loved ones)
- Makes you responsible for their happiness, stability, contentment
- Is jealous of attention you pay to others

COERCIVE CONTROL STRATEGIES WIELDED TOWARD LESBIAN, GAY, PLURISEXUAL, TRANS, AND NONBINARY INDIVIDUALS

This list of power and control tactics is created by FORGE Forward, a website with a ton of great resources for trans people. Dr. Faith has found that many items on the list apply to relationships in which at least one person is not heterosexual, even if they are cisgender. Their list, with her additions based on her clinical experiences and the experiences of her friends, is below:

- Disregarding, diminishing, disrespecting your identity (names, pronouns, etc).
- Making fun of or belittling these same identity markers
- Ridiculing your appearance
- Denying your identity (that you are not a real man, woman, enby, etc.)

- Using pejorative terms to describe you identity or aspects of your identity (including terms for body parts)
- Telling you no one will love you
- Telling you you are an embarrassment to communities to which you belong (LGBT community, church community, your bowling league, etc.)
- Refusing to let you discuss issues specific to your identity
- Threatening to out you to individuals you are not yet out to
- Weaponizing others' negative feelings about you to hurt you (e.g., having a fundamentalist preacher try to "save" you)
- Weaponizing the healthcare system or judicial system against you (threatening mental health commitments, police action, etc.)
- Restricting or denying access to medical affirmative care (therapy, hormones, surgery)
- Restricting or denying access to personal affirmative items (clothing, prosthetics, etc.)
- Fetishizing your body

GREEN FLAGS

After reading those really dreary lists of all of the terrible ways that someone that you love might be treating you or someone else that you love, let's visit some good signs of a healthy relationship. A partner in a healthy relationship:

- Helps you feel safe expressing yourself
- Respects your answers even if it's not what they want to hear
- Asks questions to better understand your perspective
- Laughs at your jokes
- Asks you for your opinion and is engaged with the answers

- Listens without giving advice (unless asked)
- Sets and keeps boundaries
- Respects your boundaries
- Takes an interest in your interests
- Is honest with themselves
- Responds rather than reacts
- Accepts your emotions instead of invalidating or dismissing them
- Admits when they were wrong
- Is open to new things, curious about new ideas, and non-judgmental towards others' choices
- Knows their own feelings and keeps them separate from yours
- Supports your personal growth
- Does not withhold love and affection to punish you
- Is comfortable doing their own things separately
- Does not leave you feeling the need to prove yourself
- Makes you feel communicated with
- Is positive and supportive towards you even when you are not positive or being supportive
- Makes for enjoyable company.
- Accepts your past without judgement
- Makes an effort to get to know your family and friends
- Does not expect to be the center of your universe
- Does not compare you to others

CONCLUSION

Congratulations. You've just slogged through a tremendous amount of information. You may want to revisit this book or various chapters periodically as you reach various stages in various relationships. Remember, the most important part of a relationship is creating and agreeing on a set of mutually accepted and respected guidelines. These guidelines should make all parties happy, emotionally fulfilled, and able to grow as people; a sum that is greater than its individual parts. Relationships save lives and help us move towards our meaning and purpose. They help us to see things that are important to us that we couldn't figure out on our own. Relationships are always about more than just sex and are never about bending people to our will or doing our bidding. Don't let your friend or partner treat you like they are your parent, and don't treat them like they are your child. Relationships are a deeply two-way street where we also learn to understand our own hang-ups and childhood trauma—and work through it all—together.

To make it through difficult situations, keep your coping skills ready to utilize. And rely on your relationships when you are unsure how to cope. Even when you disagree with people that you are close to, those conflicts are almost always the best opportunities for growth and becoming closer.

And again, life is about learning from a series of experiences. That's not to suggest that they won't be painless, particularly as they will often involve isolation and loneliness at times, but through forming lasting relationships you can literally save lives, including your own! And remember, the most common problem in neurologically mixed relationships is not understanding what the other person is trying to express.

So get out there (if you want to) and start having experiences!

FURTHER READING

- *Life and Love: Positive Strategies for Autistic Adults* (Zosia Zaks)—an autistic woman's perspective on all aspects of humaning.

- *Aspie Girl's Guide to Being Safe with Men: The Unwritten Safety Rules That No One is Telling You* (Debbie Brown)—illuminating in many ways but inferior to *Life and Love* in being less definitive and lacking exposition.

- *Asperger's Syndrome and Long-Term Relationships* (Ashley Stanford)—a somewhat hateful allistic perspective on dating us that might be illuminating for understanding how allistics talk about us behind closed doors.

- *Love and Asperger's: Practical Strategies To Help Couples Understand Each Other and Strengthen Their Connection* (Kate McNulty) Very introductory guide on couples relationships in counseling and conflict resolution.

- *Sex Without Roles: Transcending Gender* (Eli Sachse) A guide by a trans man on how gender impacts our sex lives subconsciously.

- *22 Things a Woman Must Know If She Loves a Man with Asperger's Syndrome* (Rudy Simone) An autistic guide that focuses on many of the relational dynamic aspects of relationships with many examples.

- *22 Things a Woman with Asperger's Syndrome Wants Her Partner to Know* (Rudy Simone) An autistic guide that focuses on many of the relational dynamic aspects of relationships with many examples.

- *Love In Abundance: A Counselor's Advice on Open Relationships* (Kathy Labriola).

- *Unfuck Your Boundaries: Build Better Relationships Through Consent, Communication, and Expressing Your Needs* (Dr. Faith Harper).

- *Unfuck Your Boundaries Workbook: Build Better Relationships Through Consent, Communication, and Expressing Your Needs* (Dr. Faith Harper).

- *Unfuck Your Intimacy: Using Science for Better Relationships, Sex, and Dating* (Dr. Faith Harper).

- *Unfuck Your Intimacy Workbook: Using Science for Better Relationships, Sex, and Dating* (Dr. Faith Harper).

- *How to Be Accountable: Take Responsibility to Change Your Behavior, Boundaries, and Relationships* (Joe Biel and Dr. Faith Harper) .

- *BDSM FAQ: Your Antidote to Fifty Shades of Grey* (Dr. Faith Harper).

- *The Autism Handbook: Understand Its Many Intricacies* (Joe Biel and Dr. Faith Harper).

- *The Autism Partner Handbook: How to Love Someone on the Spectrum* (Joe Biel and Dr. Faith Harper).

- *Autism and the Re:Spectrum of Human Emotions/Perfect Mix Tape Segue #6: Autism & Intellectually Understanding Empathy* (Joe Biel).

- *Proud to Be Retarded* (series edited by Joe Biel and Eliot Daughtry).

- *Your Neurodiverse Friend* (series edited by Joe Biel and Eliot Daughtry).

ABOUT THE AUTHORS

Joe Biel is a self-made autistic publisher and filmmaker who draws origins, inspiration, and methods from punk rock and has been featured in *Time Magazine, Publisher's Weekly, Oregonian, Spectator (Japan), G33K (Korea), and Maximum Rocknroll*. Biel is the author of ten books and over a hundred zines. joebiel.net

Faith Harper PhD, LPC-S, ACS, ACN is a bad-ass, funny lady with a PhD. She's a licensed professional counselor, board supervisor, certified sexologist, and applied clinical nutritionist with a private practice and consulting business in San Antonio, TX. She has been an adjunct professor and a TEDx presenter, and proudly identifies as a woman of color and uppity intersectional feminist. She is the author of dozens of books.

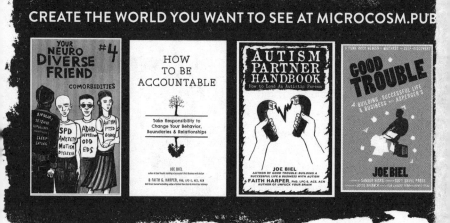